*Reality of*
*Occult/Yoga/Meditation/Flying Saucers*

*Also by Rex Dutta*

FLYING SAUCER VIEWPOINT
FLYING SAUCER MESSAGE

# Reality of
# Occult/Yoga/Meditation/Flying Saucers

## Rex Dutta

PELHAM BOOKS

First published in Great Britain by Pelham Books Ltd
52 Bedford Square, London WC1B 3EF
1974

© 1974 by Rex Dutta

ISBN 0 7207 0789 7

Set and printed in Great Britain by
Tonbridge Printers Ltd, Peach Hall Works, Tonbridge, Kent
in Times eleven on twelve point on paper supplied by
P. F. Bingham Ltd, and bound by Dorstel Press,
Harlow

# Dedication

To all who serve humanity

– – – – – – –

calling 'People of the Web'

– – –

# Foreword

This book is an elementary introduction to the teachings
of Madame Blavatsky prepared by a group of English
students. While elementary, it nevertheless is incisive in
elucidating Key elements of her teachings which should be
instructive for contemporary needs. While the tone of
instruction may at times have the sting of the gadfly, it
does have an awakening effect. There is special value in
the presentation of the modern UFO evidence as well as of
the Geller effect as these relate to more traditional
knowledge. As a first step out of the mundane way of life
the reader will find this work a reliable map towards a
richer journey into the future.

**Andrija Puharich**

# Contents

Part One  OCCULT

## Part Two YOGA

## Part Three MEDITATION

## Part Four FLYING SAUCERS

# PART ONE

# *OCCULT*

## Essential

You, the reader, how are you going to approach this book, for all depends on your own attitude and conditioning as to the genuine open-ness in the long path to Truth. Ancient Truth. Timeless Truth. Way beyond the confines of 'this village, planet earth' and of dense physical earthlings of five-only senses. A moment's thought will surely bring the realization that Realities must inevitably be grander and older than us and ours; the multifold galaxies that abound visibly, tangibly, pull us magnetically to wider horizons, and make essential that too-limited bonds be shed, that the conscious knowledge of man expand.

There are far more habitable planets in our local star-areas than there are houses here on our mud-speck, teeming forms of Life, not necessarily limited to our dense standard, to our parochial ideas; in expressions and powers and attributes far far beyond the familiar.

To understand the Galaxies it is we who have to rise in stature; not scream that they come down to our size. It's time to grow. Let's start now.

# 1. Whence Separation?
# Whence this physical body?

LET'S hope, let's help each other, to maintain the resolve
– essential – just outlined. Without it, understanding will
be insufficient, partial, blocked – more accurately deserving
the description of prejudice, albeit unconscious.

What then is the main handicap to this fuller
understanding of Truth?

A dense physical body, which we tend to mistake as
'me'; as a thing very separate from 'you'.

This separation has caused all manner of blind spots:
we have divided off into male-female, religion-science,
god-devil, objective-subjective, and worst of all have
become so dulled that we regard this stupid viewpoint as
normal, as inevitable – the very concept of balance, of
whole-ness, of One-ness have been banished into the realms
of metaphysical speculations – and we do not even seem
to notice that when we walk (we actually have the cheek to
be proud of the 'gracefulness' of our walk!) we waddle to
the left of the point of balance or to the right as we jerk
along on our two differentiated legs and rarely maintain
poised equilibrium. Uneven-ness is also the hallmark of
our breath – the very source of our physical life – as we
either breathe in or out and blithely are unconcerned that
we fail utterly to remain at the mid-point of neither in nor

out, that is, at All-Breath.

Arguing that all this lop-sided stuff is natural, the more encrusted of us dismiss outright as 'impossible' the persistent accounts through the thousands of centuries of people who 'glided along' (even going through solid brick walls), or of Eastern yogis who could be buried alive without air for days or weeks or months and who attained the poise of 'All-Breath' and not merely survived, but thrived. During the past short decade this ability has been proved too often under rigorous test conditions to be denied, even by the obdurate, and yet still gets shrugged off as 'trance' – a vaguely dead state not really worthy of us practical-and-sensible folk. We could be wrong. Very wrong.

Anyway, how did earthling humanity get this wobbly little body in the first place? Fragmented off into two arms (that flap to the left or to the right), two ears, two eyes, two nostrils – at least we had the inner sense to keep one head, to give us a chance to lead ourselves back to One-ness, that's if we bother with such out-of-the-rut considerations.

So, where did this body come from? The answer depends of course on which separated fragment we ask. If we're staggering around bearing the proud load of Western Science – somehow capital letters always seem appropriate – then we're stuck with Darwin and a couple of apes; we're also stuck with an enormous flaw that makes the whole concept collapse but we slide round that by elevating it into a grandiose 'missing link'. And the conclusion of this nuts and bolts, outer-form only, ignoring the inner (and unprovable) factors of feelings / Life / thoughts – is that this form is the apex, the culmination, that is, we are magnificent-animals. But animals, just the same.

Ask the same question from another fragment, generally labelled religious, and our body is alleged to have been delivered ready-made from some benign Sugar-Daddy 'up there'. It sort of, kinda came, complete with its male-female divisions, and with (only) its five little senses, all neatly packaged. And *why* only five senses? Oh, don't ask! or Sugar-Daddy said five was enough. The title of the 'up there' matters little, there are a dozen or more scattered around (Jesus, Allah, Krishna, Zoroaster, Troth, Osiris, Narayama of Atlantis, etc. etc.), but why in the name of common sense does it have to be a He? Why not She? or It? or at least 'That' from which Itness comes. How can One-ness have a gender? Or a form?

*Did any of the above facetiousness irritate you? If so* why? What is *your* prejudice? A truth seeker might have recognized the inner validity of the probing – however poorly done – and would have tended to bring to life the first paragraph of this chapter; it could only be the encrusted who tend first, foremost, above all, to defend the separated fragment.

Prejudice is a big word.

So let us consider, the occult version of where this body came from.

# 2. The Occult

First, what is Occult? Basically it is beyond the outer-form, the temporal, the evanescent; ever seeking the noumenon rather than the phenomenon, the cause not the effect, the within and not merely the without. Layer after layer – timeless, spaceless. States of consciousness – ever more deeply/exactly knowable and attainable gradations of positive KNOWLEDGE. Repeat – knowledge not belief. Nothing should be taken on trust; all should be tested and proved by each individual aspirant.

But how to test? How to know? How to develop the faculties necessary? Much study and perseverence are pre-requisite – or course, how else could you be a surgeon/a nuclear physicist/a Shakespeare, a Bach, a Pythagoras – but all are attainable by all, in one life or another.

Meanwhile popular (uninformed) prejudice against 'the occult' abounds, and smears up as a hotchpotch of black magic, voodoo, hallucination, devil. Yet the modern giants of Science, men like Sir John Eccles, Wolfgang Pauli, Henry Marganau, and their predecessors, take it very seriously, as do a markedly high proportion of Nobel Prizewinners; it is the second-raters that cling to their nuts and bolts. Truly religious aspirants, who can break out of the blinkers of some particular 'holy book' to One-ness, also take occultism very seriously, even though they suffer the shrug-off as mystic – misty seeing. Yet their examples over the years have encouraged humanity in its millions to loosen its bonds, and to seek, to investigate, ever brightening the hope for the future.

So, how do the Occultists say you got your body, and your five senses?

Refusing the division of life and form, the Occultists insist on One-ness, where both life/form 'are'; but latent, un-knowing, not yet self conscious. This is a main stumbling block to both the scientist and to the parson: the former believes (he does not know) that the original impulse/source is not conscious – where is the science text-book that speaks of Mr Electricity, Mr Heat, Mr Moisture, Mr Gravity, Mr Magnetism; and the parson believes (he does not know) that the original impulse/source is all-good, all-knowing, etc., instead of *potentially* the origin of both the good-bad, seen-unseen, etc.

Until the parson and the scientist get beyond nuts and bolts and the five-only senses, neither are sure – but both will argue; and will unite in their hearty condemnation of the fool of an occultist.

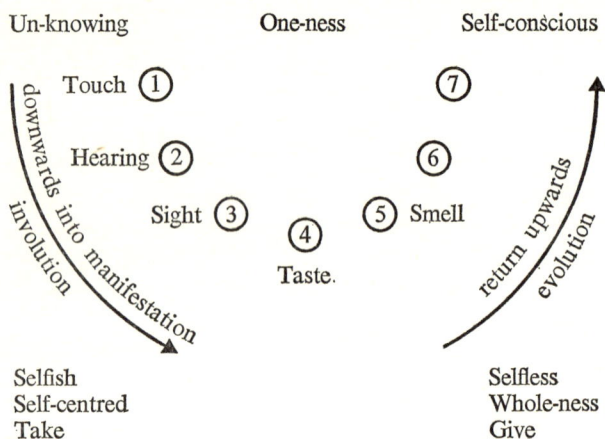

Un-knowing     One-ness     Self-conscious

downwards into manifestation involution

Touch ①  
Hearing ②  
Sight ③  
④ Taste.  
⑤ Smell  
⑥  
⑦  

return upwards evolution

Selfish  
Self-centred  
Take

Selfless  
Whole-ness  
Give

The inherent quality of Motion carries One-ness 'downwards' into manifestation, and then 'upwards' back to One-ness *plus* all the fruits of experience as the downward arc of involution is replaced by the upward return arc of evolution; the whole being classified into

**18**

seven great stages, or steps, or Root Races (technical term) – one of our body senses being developed in each Root Race. Each Root Race having seven by seven main subdivisions and taking the duration of a Round (technical term) for birth, fruition, death; the whole seven Rounds forming one Manvantara (technical term) that is, 4,320,000,000 earthling years or the 'eternity' of a Christian.

At the moment we are in the Fifth Root Race, and have been for a million years, and have five senses – two more being undeveloped as yet.

Also by now the scientist and the parson will be speechless with rage / damnation. However, to continue:


SECTION 1. *Touch*

Considering at first merely the development of the physical body of earthlings, the first 'veiling' took place in the First Root Race, who were largely unconscious and formless – solely producing over aeons of time a vague awareness depicted as a sense of touch. Yet the sense was close to One-ness, or whole-ness, and to this day we respond no matter which (all-over) part of our body is touched. That's at the outer, or physical level; at the inmost meditators use words like Seventh Samadhi, Initiates use Liberation / Nirvana / Supreme, and mystics talk of he-gods, Rohanee, Omnipresent, etc. – all groping towards 'state seven', as yet 'not-developed', and not yet reached by any earthling, not even the Gautama Buddha who is said to be the finest flowering yet. (Irate adherents to other title-holders of 'up there' please please restrain your thunderbolts.)


SECTION 2. *Hearing*

Specialization, that is, differentiation, started in the Second Root Race, yet another 'veiling', densified the unconscious formless all-over First Race into loose / tenuous / somewhat invisible 'cloud-like' beginning-to-be-recognisable forms of the Second Root Race. Separating

19

forms, the forerunners of (you separate from me) things that now litter this planet, and now we can hear only with our ears. So the nuts and bolts specialists say; an occultist says that there are seven ears (five inner) and by using them you can hear with any part of your body (or none!) at distances in space and time that are incredulous to a mere five-senser. Yet we millions of five-sensers grope after these with artificial aids, like the telephone, the megaphone, the amplifier, and vaguely are beginning to start to commence to come around to considering the weird concept that peoples of other planets may not be as restricted (even in hearing) as we are. Space Travellers have long demonstrated the proof; even 'our books' speak of having ears to hear! Hence all those stories of 'my He-God can hear whatever is said anywhere, or can hear my secret thoughts.'

The Sixth Round yet to come corresponds to the Second and will see the perfecting of the qualities of hearing originated in the early beginnings of the Second Round. Starting with the faculty of hearing, full development will go through the intense-animal hearing on the physical plane of the most skilled jungle-type man, up into the inner ears of Omniscience, i.e. All-hearing, i.e. All Knowing of all 'things' such as not only of sounds (however distant) but of thoughts, even colours. The Russian Government set up four scientific institutes in 1965 to study these manifestations and it is high time we followed suit. All of us multi-millions, by then (the Sixth Race) being full six-sensers will then do what one – the Buddha – has now done, as an earthling. Out in the multifold galaxies many are the Space Peoples who are at this stage. Do not 'our books' say that there are many mansions in my Father's house.

Of course, we will never do it with just nuts and bolts; nor by argument. We need (a) to grow (b) to develop the inner faculties and then (c) to test. But stage (a) and stage (b) simply cannot be skipped if ever we are to become, or even be able to understand, "clairaudience' – clear hearing, that is, all-hearing. Space Peoples are not lumbered with primitive telephones plus tangled wires!

20

SECTION 3. *Sight*

The Third Root Race developed sight. The tenuous-cloud-like forms of the Second Root Race increased their separation/densification over the huge spans of cosmic time, until finally the planet earth settled nearer its present state and on to modern geological time. An earthling race – the Third – flourished some 18 million to 5 million B.C. in a land now sunk under the Pacific Ocean, and which occultists call Lemuria. The Race was 'tenuous' and was struggling to unite spirit-matter as increased veiling of the One-ness began to become recognizable as 'matter', albeit not yet solid. Tall, loose and inchoate these were the giants of mythology, at first with the single eye in the centre of the head, but gradually densifying into the dual eyes, recognizable today. In this narrative the focus is on the physical body – other important aspects being left till later – but it has now to be noted that parallel developments to the dual eyes included (*a*) dual substance, that is, spirit conjoining with matter to establish stability (*b*) spiritual inner faculties being overlaid with veiling to give densified outer forms which became conscious of being separate, in the sense of being 'distinct' or 'apart', and hence the forerunner of selfishness, that is, sense of separateness (*c*) hence the dividing of the ways, for example, left and right hand path, black and white magic, etc.

All the exoteric religions of the past few hundreds of thousands of years have tended to allegorize this Lemurian period as the fall of man. For in truth this is where physical generation began: simultaneous with the separation into duality was included the duality of the sexes. Yet traces of One-ness persist, and today the most masculine of men have female hormones in their own bodies; for the good reason that humanity will re-unite its dualities in the coming Sixth Root Race to become again Androgyne – male-female as one. But of that, more presently.

The separation into the two sexes was accomplished in four stages, and this transition period lasted from 18 million to 6 million B.C., leaving the Third Root Race to flower and die 6 million to 5 million B.C. Of course the time scale is approximate, yet far more accurate than some

21

would allow. Not even the most obdurate now claims that creation took place 4004 B.C. – the date printed on Christian bibles only a short 50 years ago. Esoteric reading of the 'six days of creation' as the six Root Races, with the seventh as a day of rest, meaning the perfection of the Seventh Root Race, would be far nearer truth. More intelligent, too, would be a reading of '4004 years' as (1) the creation of the four elements (fire, air, water, earth) on the one hand, to give the beginnings of the 'four corners of the earth whence we shall be gathered together', the square of the Freemasons, the cube of the Moslems; and (2) simultaneous with the four Rounds (technical term) of time during which these developments took place. The two noughts in the centre speaking of 'two' parallel developments in space and in motion of even more vast concepts linking this tiny planet to the galaxies.

The four stages of the separation of the sexes from the original unified Hermaphrodite were : (1) Budding – as the largely-unconscious 'forms' remaining from the Second Root Race just split off; as still do today our lower echelons of life like some plants, moluscs and cells. (2) Extrusion – as the life-essence was forced out into space / time, rather like ectoplasm from a medium in a seance, there to become 'separate'. (3) Sweat-born – as the extrusion was done not passively, that is, unconsciously, but actively / knowingly as 'WILL' began to densify and project (parallel with 'spirit' and with 'matter'). (4) The Egg-Born – when the conscious 'sweat' became directed and focused to a degree not previously possible – because simultaneously the vaguer sight of the single central eye was sharpened into the dual externalized eyes.

Thence, came the last step – into distinct separation of the sexes, as still exists.

So now humanity had three senses – Touch, Hearing, Sight; had begun to conjoin in stability the two 'separate branches of One-ness' called spirit and matter and so to acquire a recognizable body; and duality, that is, separation existed – hence also the beginning of conscious individualism as 'I am I', as 'The Fall', as Selfishness. Humanity began to take (rather than be at-one), began to

be self-seeking, began wars. The three stages of the trinity
had reached the definitive point of the son; the pilgrim
on his way through numerous incarnations round the Wheel
of Rebirth, the prodigal son now well out from home
before he could return. This too was the stage of the
'missing link' of Darwin, erroneous because nuts-and-bolts
science deliberately excludes from its field of research the
'spiritual', even thoughts or feelings; concentrating uniquely
on the outer form, on matter – which simply did not
'exist' in earlier Lemuria, that is, had not been sufficiently
densified to be within the (dense) range of microscopes,
carbon dating and the like. Interesting, though, are the
physical skulls, like the one discovered by Professor
Leakey, which belong to late Lemurian times, that is, to
'solidified matter'.


SECTION 4. *Taste*

Overlapping Lemuria came the Fourth Root Race – that
of Atlantis – which flourished 5 million to 1 million B.C.
and which developed the fourth earthling body sense, that
of taste. Atlanteans used to bury their meat till it became
'high', the more to enjoy the developing faculty of taste;
remnant earthlings to this day, overdo the spices / sauces /
gorgonzola / high meats!

Densification increased apace, speech developed, so did
city and nation civilizations, crafts and cultures, and
engineering feats we still cannot emulate (conceited
scientists please don't get too cross). Using the 'night side
of Nature' – the darker shadow of the occult forces now
derided by some, they had weapons and technology far
beyond the cobalt bomb or the orbiting missile. Increasingly
does modern research prove that we are merely re-inventing
lost arts. Let us consider for a moment the following solid
home-truths:

(1) At Baalbeck exist single blocks of stone weighing
2,000 tons each. How could we cut such blocks from a
quarry; how could we lift them into position?

(2) In Peru, similar blocks still stand in edifices on the
mountain top; the quarries being thousands of feet in the

valleys below.

(3) Also in South America exist ground markings ranging over hundreds of square miles, totally meaningless from low down but from about 50,000 feet stretching out clearly as 'airfield landing markers'.

(4) Worked-jewels/gold found slap in the middle of coal seams, millenia old; clear relics of electric batteries; murals, lost dyes, optical lenses; Stonehenge and the Great Pyramid demonstrating exact astronomical knowledge, and clearly showing the altered positions of the pole stars; all of an antiquity when earthlings were supposed to be scratching about with stone/bronze/iron implements.

So simple is the basic explanation of these 'scientific irregularities' that the encrusted try to sweep under the carpet and forget – the continents did not 'drift apart on plates' but rose and submerged. As Lemuria sank under the Pacific, Atlantis rose out of the Atlantic; when it sank (in four stages and over a span of 850,000 years) modern continents and seas settled as they now are. Recognition of this simple fact radically will alter our dating theories. Let us, too, get a better picture of the allegories of the Flood, of all the exoteric religions of every continent, every culture. Atlantis in its hey-day covered far more than just the present sea, included huge slabs of modern North America and Africa: 850,000 B.C. the first of the floods, lasting in spasms to 200,000 B.C. had reduced it to the 'Atlantic'; by 85,000 B.C. this had been split into the two islands of Ruta and Daitya; which then sank and left the single shrunken island of Poseidonis; finally destroyed in the last of the great Floods in 9564 B.C. (Sorry about 'the Minoan civilization at Crete' which the nuts-and-bolts chaps are trying to palm of as a 'possible' Atlantis.)

So in this Atlantean Fourth Root Race we densified down till 'matter overcame spirit', reducing our physical height from fifteen feet to twelve to eight (relics also prove this although 'explained away' as the skeletons of animals), 'lost' our spiritual connection with One-ness, and reached the densest point of the involutionary arc.

The turning point had been reached.

Let us please notice a curious but vital trend.

The first faculty of Touch was intensely local, limited to the 'being' (the future man) and was passive; evoked only and solely when he was touched – from the outside. One-ness had become focused / manifested / outpoured.

The second faculty of Hearing took the 'future man' out of his shell / form so that he could respond to distant stimuli and not merely to direct touch. In fact the sounds could travel through solid brick walls to reach him; his range (and penetration) of response had vastly increased.

At the third stage, Sight began to be limited in the sense that man could no longer see through a solid brick wall; at least, not with his externalized dual and separated eyes, although his inner eye could do that and much more, as Space Peoples, Initiates, Yogis, and others demonstrate repeatedly over spans of time for those 'who have eyes to see'. Dense physical man was 'contracting' into his own centre, forming a separated selfish unit apart from others, that is, from One-ness.

Taste, the fourth faculty, carried this selfishness to the extreme: food held even one inch away from the mouth could not be tasted (the faculty of smell had not yet been acquired). It was as self-centred as man could get.

Came the turning point, the ending of the involution-into-matter downwards arc: we can now smell beyond that hitherto-limiting brick wall. The Return arc of evolution-back-to-One-ness has begun.

The time scale is of an immense grandeur worthy of Truth, and enormous overlaps exist – do we still not take tomato ketchup with almost everything, do we still not drink hot coffee after cold ice-cream! Many too are the really important facets that have been deliberately omitted in order to maintain this concentration on the earthling physical body; some are dealt with later; for the others, cordially are serious investigators invited to contact the author. So too are the critics.

## Section 5. *Smell*

So at last we come to modern five-sensed man, a million years old.

Early on it was mentioned that each great Root Race had seven by seven main divisions, and our Aryan Fifth Root Race had these:

(*a*) Aryan Root Stock. Still surviving, as in India, and still showing clear traces of a mind particularly able to grasp instantly deep metaphysical aspects and of an inner balance that manifests as beauty of the features and of the hands.

(*b*) The Persian – not the modern remnants, though Eastern peoples have long tended to regard the cultural heritage of this sub-root Race in the same way that Westerners regard Ancient Greece and Rome.

(*c*) The Chaldees. Now almost totally lost to history, as indeed are the 'Persians', and during whose culture white magic reached its highest (densified) perfection yet on our planet.

The occult description of the second and third sub-root Races, purposely veiled in allegory, is 'Sons of Ad' (a very high state of consciousness) and 'Sons of the Fire-mist' (a high state of white magic).

(*d*) The Celts – who to this day are considered 'faye', that is, as responsive to the subtle elemental forces of nature, allegorized as fairies, gnomes and so forth. The vital difference being that conscious control of these more subtle/inner forces has been lost in the absence of detailed knowledge of the gradations/immediate and full ability to co-work with them.

(*e*) The Nordic, or Caucasian with a magnificent concrete brain, superb at the nuts-and-bolts level. Look at the externalization of the inner senses he had done: for inner touch – outer instruments, sensitive to a degree; for inner hearing – the outer telephone/electronic bugging devices; for inner sight – outer telescopes; for inner smell and inner taste (fragrance/music of colours) – the externalized gadgets are only being produced as yet.

When this superb concrete brain of the fifth sub-root Race (excellent for war, for administration, for business organization) is fused with the metaphysical ability of the first sub-root Aryan stock, then will develop the sixth sub-root Race, in several thousand earthling years yet to come. The forerunners can be dimly sensed, for example in North America (and elsewhere of course) as humanity responds to telepathy, the Extra Sensory Perception, to moving solid objects with the power of thought (psychokinetics), and starts following the example of its scientific giants (not the second-raters) and actually investigates, rather than sneers at, clairvoyance/ clairaudience/clairsentience – in short the precursors of the 'New Age' qualities of our future Races.

Western peoples are sure to ask what happened to Ancient Greece and to Rome, the source of so much culture, and can be incredulously disbelieving to have them dismissed as sub-sub races of very limited consequence in the time scale now being outlined. Even more amazing to their current concepts is the bland assertion that these four sub-root civilizations were flowering during the past million years, when god-fearing honest folk plus the educated/objective/authoritative scientists both combine in the belief that 'it was more or less dark' before Jerusalem. Such prejudice being nowhere sustained; but being everywhere recognizable.

Would you like to consider the book from which extracts are now given below?

*The Mahatma Letters to A. P. Sinnett.* Written 1882, published 1923. From Letter xxiiib:

'Yes; the fifth race – ours – began in Asia a million years ago. What was it about for the 998,000 years preceding the last 2000? A pertinent question; offered moreover in quite a Christian spirit that refuses to believe that any good could ever have come from anywhere *before* and *save* Nazareth. What was it about? . . . No doubt your geologists are very learned; but why not bear in mind that, under the continents explored and fathomed by them, in the bowels of which they have found the "Eocene Age" (penned 1882) and forced it to deliver them its secrets, there may be, hidden deep in the fathomless, or rather unfathomed ocean beds, other, and far older continents whose stratums have never been geologically explored; and that they may some day upset entirely their present theories, thus illustrating the simplicity and sublimity of truth as connected with inductive "generalization" in opposition to their visionary conjectures. Why not admit – true no one of them has ever thought of it – that our *present* continents, have like "Lemuria" and "Atlantis" – been *several times already* submerged and had the time to re-appear again, to bear their new groups of mankind and civilization; and that, at the first great geological upheaval at the next cataclysm – in the series of periodical cataclysms that occur from the beginning to end of every Round (technical term) – our already *autopsized* continents will go down, and Lemuria and Atlantis come up again. Think of future geologists of the sixth and seventh Races. Imagine them digging in the bowels of what was Ceylon and Simla, and finding implements of the Veddahs or of the remote ancestors of the *civilized* Pahari – every object of the civilized portions of humanity that inhabited those regions having been pulverized to dust by the great masses of travelling glaciers – during the next glacial period – imagine them finding only such rude implements as are now found among those savage tribes; and forthwith declaring that during that period *primitive* man climbed and slept on the trees, and sucked the marrow out of animal bones after breaking them . . .'

'Of course the Fourth Race had its periods of the highest civilizations. Greek and Roman and even Egyptian civilizations are nothing compared to the civilizations that began with the Third Race . . . Greeks and Romans were small *sub-races,* and the Egyptians part and parcel of our own "Caucasian" stock. Look at the latter and at India. Having reached the highest civilization and what is more : *learning* – both went down. Egypt was a distinct sub-race disappearing entirely (her Copts are a hybrid remnant). India – as one of the first and most powerful off-shoots of the mother Race, and composed of a number of sub-races – lasting to these times, and struggling to take

28

once more her place in history some day. That History catches but a few stray, hazy glimpses of Egypt, some 12,000 years back; when, having already reached the apex of its cycle thousands of years before, the latter had begun going down. What does, or *can* it know of India 5,000 years ago, or of the Chaldees – whom it confounds most charmingly with the Assyrians, making of them one day "Akkadians", at another Turanians and what not? We say then, that your History is entirely at sea.'

'. . . Do you know that the Chaldees were at the apex of their Occult fame *before* what you term as the "bronze age"? That the "Sons of Ad" or the children of the Fire-mist preceded by hundreds of centuries the Age of Iron, which was an old age already, when what you now call the Historical Period – probably because what is known of it is generally no history but fiction – had hardly begun. We hold – but then what warrant can you give the world that we are right? – that far "greater civilizations than our own have risen and decayed". It is not enough to say as some of your modern writers do – that an extinct civilization existed before Rome and Athens were founded. We affirm that a *series* of civilizations existed *before*, as well as after the Glacial Period, that they existed upon various points of the globe, reached the apex of glory – and died. Every trace and memory had been lost of the Assyrian and Phoenicean civilizations until discoveries began to be made a few years ago. (Penned 1882). And now they open a new, though not by far one of the earliest pages in the history of mankind. And yet how far back do those civilizations go in comparison with the oldest? – and even them, history is shy to accept. Archaeology has sufficiently demonstrated that the memory of man runs back vastly further than history has been willing to accept, and the sacred records of once mighty nations preserved by their heirs are still more worthy of trust. We speak of civilizations of the ante-glacial period; and (not only in the minds of the vulgar and the profane but even in the opinion of the highly learned geologist) the claim sounds preposterous. What would you say then to our affirmation that the

29

Chinese – I now speak of the inland, the true Chinaman, not the hybrid mixture between the fourth and fifth Races now occupying the throne – the aborigines, who belong in their unallied nationality wholly to the last and highest branch of the Fourth Race, reached their highest civilization when the Fifth had hardly appeared in Asia, and that its first off-shoot was yet a thing of the future. When was it? Calculate. (more than 1 million years ago).'

'. . . The group of islands off the Siberian coast discovered by Nordeneskjol of the "Vega" was found strewn with fossils of horses, sheep, oxen, etc., among gigantic bones of elephants, mammoths, rhinoceroses, and other monsters belonging to periods when man – says your science – had not yet made his appearance on earth. How came horses and sheep to be found in company with huge "ante-diluvians"? The horse, we are taught in schools – is quite a modern invention of nature, and *no man* ever saw its pedactyl ancestor. The group of Siberian islands may give the lie to the comfortable theory. The region now locked in the fetters of eternal winter uninhabited by man – that most fragile of animals – will be very soon proved to have had not only a tropical climate – something that your science knows and does not dispute – but having been likewise the seat of one of the most ancient civilizations of that Fourth Race whose highest relics now we find in the degenerated Chinaman, and whose lowest are hopelessly (for the profane scientist) intermixed with the remnants of the Third. I told you before now, that the highest people now on earth (spiritually) belong to the first sub-race of the Fifth Root Race; and those are the Aryan Asiatics; the highest race (physical intellectuality) is the last sub-race of the Fifth – yourselves, the white conquerors . . .'

Would you, the serious reader, have realized that those words were penned in 1882? Did you not find the style to be timeless?

Do you really think such writings should deserve the popular prejudice of 'the occult being a hotch-potch of black-magic, voodoo, hallucination, devil'.

There are 150 such letters (many are short), published as shown at the end of this book. We have quoted less than an eighth of one.

Let's hope it encourages you, the serious student, to investigate further.

# 3. Preliminaries to understanding the Powers of Mind over Matter

*How many lives?*

The sevenfold stages that developed our physical body and its senses, have far wider repercussions, of course. Also they keynote the seven states of consciousness we seek to master with each of our seven 'bodies', often considered thus:

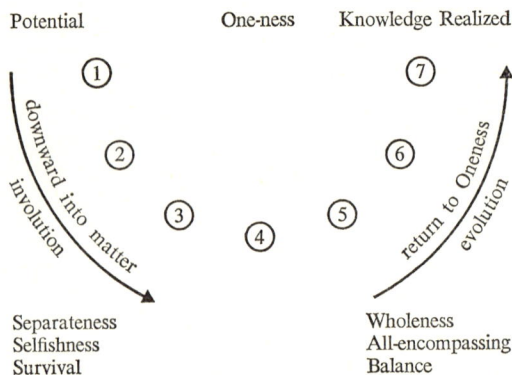

Potential      One-ness      Knowledge Realized

downward into matter / involution

return to Oneness / evolution

① ② ③ ④ ⑤ ⑥ ⑦

Separateness
Selfishness
Survival

Wholeness
All-encompassing
Balance

'You' have seven 'bodies', it could be said. The physical thing that we all drag around, and which the more animal-like say is 'you'; but it's not you, it's a tool you use, a magnificent tool – we saw in the last chapter how

32

some 3,000 million years were needed to produce it, and you might be interested to consider that you have spent some 770 lives moulding your own. This figure is partly mathematical as we would have to incarnate at least once, often more, in each sub-sub-sub-race of a major Root Race, i.e., 4 Root Races x (7 sub x 7 sub x 7 sub-branches of a Root Race) plus the similar divisions of the present Fifth Root Race (now in its fifth sub-race, that is, the Caucasian): each sub-race having 7 divisions (like Greece / Rome, Egypt, etc.) That would total far more than 770 lives, but few of us did the whole evolutionary stretch here in this village, planet earth; most did part of the evolution in 'other mansions in my Father's house'. The allegory of the 770 is a basic 7 'twice round' as a jungle-sort of primitive, as a slower moving country type, firmly to root (and perhaps to control) the more basic instincts and faculties, at a relatively leisured pace, that is, 7 x 10 of perfection x (second time round) 10 of greater perfection = 700. Then we all begin to move into the city-Slicker state of rapid decisions (if only to evade traffic) of crowds, of multifold pressures, of wider horizons (we hope) i.e. 7 x only, once round, the 10 of perfection, that is, 70.

After the 770 lives, roughly the state of fifth sub-race (Caucasian), Fifth Root Race humanity, come the 7 lives of the aspirant who seeks his own path up the mountain top – perhaps the sort of reader who could study such a book as this. These '7' lives can be shorter / longer / harder / fuller as we each tread our way, make our mistakes and reap our reward: 'as ye sow thus shall ye reap'. Our greatest pitfall is if we get caught in some soothing syrup, some catch emotion / phrase and tend to shrug off our individual responsibility on to some saviour / guru / group and usually end up:

(a) wallowing in smug self-righteousness (if we are ineffective) or (b) as an 'occult wreck' if we have pursued a false trail (no matter how respectable / acceptable / wide-spread) and have got our 'seven bodies' out of balance: 'When two or three (interior bodies, not Smith, Jones & Brown!) are gathered together (in balance) there

I (One-ness) am'. To continue with the story of our
'seven bodies':


SECTION 2. *Seven bodies of Man*

1. *Physical* First, the dense physical, just discussed;
approximately 3,000 million years old!

2. *Etheric* Second, the 'health body' – etheric being the
technical term; sometimes also called astral – which shines
a few inches round the physical, well stretched out and
radiating when healthy, but droopy when sick or tired.
Maddening as it may seem to some, the etheric body comes
first, and is the inner mould round which is overlaid the
dense physical. According to Law, to past Karma ('as ye
sow, thus shall ye reap'), according to the lessons to be
learnt in this life – is your etheric, hence your physical.
You made it. Babbling about heredity and environment
merely starts the story too late – why did you choose those
particular parents, in those particular circumstances, for
this incarnation? That's the main consideration. As was
said right at the beginning of Chapter 2, the Occult deals
with the cause rather than the effect, the noumenon
(hidden) rather than the phenomenon (visible). The aura
(which also is sevenfold) intensifies here.
   So too do the powers of mind over matter. With the
etheric body constantly flowing magnetically round the
physical, all sorts of 'magic', all sorts of 'unexplainable'
become clear:
   *Acupuncture* for one. Nuts-and-bolts medicine cannot
possibly understand why a needle stuck into your foot in
one place would anaesthetise your lower jaw, and when
moved to an adjacent spot in the same foot would enable
your dentist painlessly to drill the teeth in the upper jaw –
But flowing etheric forces when inhibited at a 'nodal point'
by the insertion of the needle cause an effect of the next
nodal point – in this case to anaesthetise the jaw.
   What could be more simple?
   Clairvoyant sight operative in the etheric 'body' is needed

to map the nodal points, after that major surgical operations without drugs, without pain, without after effects (provided the flow of the etheric field is restored) become normal. The Chinese have long proved this; Western nuts-and-bolts 'experts' are reluctantly being dragged round to conviction by the sheer weight of repeated proofs. The Chinese culture is very very old; as was pointed out on page 30, the original source going back to the last sub-race of the Fourth Root Race (of Atlantis) or to some time before 1,000,000 B.C., when etheric sight was a common attribute among earthlings.

*Tutankhamen.* The experts have long been puzzled as to why the 'curse' on those who defiled the tomb should work (because all the excavators did, in physical fact, die in unexpected/unexplained circumstances), and also why the public should repeatedly flock in such long and patient queues to see the exhibitions in Paris, in London and elsewhere. The magnetic fascination is not explainable by normal standards; other 'old' exhibitions like the 'Jade Princess' of China, or the 'Inca Princess' of Peru do not have the same drawing power.

It's the etheric force-field, of course. Tutankhamen in its symbology, its colours, its ordered patterns, its (still undeciphered) hieroglyphics – all done under the knowing/conscious/able to co-work with Nature's subtle forces Initiates – kept its force, still does, and radiates. Time and space in these inner levels are very very 'different' from the flat linear, pastpresentfuture of the five-only sensers, who are stuck and can't even travel either forward or back in 'time'. So, too, space is different and radiating 'a few inches' can easily traverse decades and continents – as can your thought: think of Delhi and 'you're there'! Now! Or in the Delhi of 'centuries ago'. Now!

Please Mr Expert don't hop around too much in rage, but the Egyptian true Initiate magic was far older than 12,000 B.C. (see page 29) by which epoch genuine Knowledge was becoming densified and overlaid –but slavishly copying the original forms/colours/patterns preserved enough of the 'matrix of inner force' to have the effect on the auras of modern folk (who 'just like Egyptian culture') to produce the queues that puzzled the others.

*The Pyramid and Razor Blades.* Just to illustrate deeper the effect of the inner etheric on the outer physical, we take the effect 'further' – as far as an 'inanimate' (there's no such thing, of course!) razor blade. It's just barely conceivable to the enlightened that a force field could radiate round the human frame (after all, science can even photograph it by ultra-sonics; and auras have long been secretly accepted) but which of the nuts-and-bolts Pundits would have thought of sharpening old razor-blades by subjecting them to the etheric force field generated not by another human – but by a lump of plastic! The roars of disbelief can be imagined. Yet hundreds of thousands of plastic models of the Great Pyramid, made *exactly* to scale (important of course) regularly sharpen myriad razor blades each night in Czechoslovakia. Just plonk the blunt blade under the hollow model, face it East-West, and in the morning it's sharp. Unbelievable, but commercially proved true. Dr Lyall Watson in his best-selling book 'Super Nature' details this, as he does many other equally-understandable-on-the-etheric-plane, but otherwise bizarre, examples.

Even the mere form, originally occultly designed, can generate/stimulate/inhibit the force field – acupuncture, Tutankhamen, razor blades and all.

In fact, that is precisely the main snag. So easy is it for the unprepared (un-initiated) to accelerate/slow the flow – the masculine yin and the female yan – that unwanted or unpleasant results can be produced as well as the beneficial if knowledge – true/sufficient/accurate/conscious knowledge – is absent.

*Motive   Motive is all-important in Occultism.* And this vital fact will repeatedly be stressed. It is one of the main reasons why the Occult 'stayed hidden' until 'people were ready for it', that is, until people had studied and understood the immutable Laws that are there to be realized. Even earthling electricity can warm – or kill; you need to know its 'law'. The same, too, for a motor car!

So there's no reason to funk it! The cable-tow of approach should be of the right length – too much hanging

36

back in fearful withdrawal, and harmful *lack* of progress ensues and the noose tightens round the neck of the neophyte; too much rashness and the sharp point of the 'dagger' of inevitable consequence of effect-following-its-cause-in-Law will soon urge us to proper caution, proper approach.

Purity of motive, and discrimination of approach, increasingly become more vital (if that's grammatically possible) as we 'gather more of our (inner) bodies together so that I (One-ness, i.e. operative magic) am.'
*Laying on of hands, and magnetic healing* are familiar to all. They work. Often. Because so very frequently the motive is relatively pure (a desire to heal/help) the etheric force field activates more readily; the etheric 'follows thought', that is whole thoughts of One-ness/Selflessness, as distinct from separated/mercenary things of 'lower down'. Further explanations become apparent in subsequent sections, but suffice now to realize that the flowing force-field of the etheric of the healer, being connected both with that of the patient and with One-ness (physical space/time being quiescent in this field) it becomes easy to understand (*a*) why cures take place (*b*) why relapses occur 'when the (etheric) link is broken/diminished (*c*) why most healers maintain that they are only channels through which force (or some He-god) surges. Happy will be the day when the healers (and their critics) will have adequate knowledge of occult LAW to be able to co-work with the etheric and other bodies *in full consciousness*.


3. *Emotion body* Motion of itself is pure movement, the very throb of the universe, and as an inherent quality is neither good nor bad – for example, electricity or gravity are 'neuter' and become either harmful or beneficial according to the use to which they are put by Man, the Thinker. Hence, too, the addition of the letter 'e', the fifth in the alphabet (the mental, see below), twists pure/unconscious/neuter motion into the good/bad emotion that we all know so well.

This motion-with-knowledge we call emotion, because

the fifth plane of occultism is the mind plane, and hence its name of Kama-Manas (technical term), that is, Kama, or Desire, plus Manas, or Mind – often only lower mind as our emotions stay personalized! Please remember that Kama (Desire) is quite different from Karma (The Law of 'as ye sow thus shall ye reap'). Also please consider that it is not feasible for us to have a thought without feeling, or a feeling without thought, except in states of rarer consciousness, hence the linking of the two as Kama-Manas, the emotional body.

Do you notice, dear reader, the compliment you are now being paid – of being moved up several grades to that of serious researcher, who welcomes technical depths which a casual surface-skimmer would not.

This e-motional, desire, body of 'I' like / 'I' want / 'I' dislike clearly is coloured by the lower mind (Manas) of the personal thoughts and feelings and deserves its technical name of Kama-Manas. It is powerful. Even on the outer planes we see the surging force of a football crowd emotionally roused; and also of a 'devotional congregation' spurred on by the thought-form of its own particularized He-god – in hate against a different He-god – as Arab-Jew, Hindu-Muslem, Protestant-Catholic; do we not all remember the vicious wars when group A begged its own He-god (loving, compassionate, all-merciful) to slaughter group B. Sticking voodoo pins in the enemy effigy is child's play to the gigantic murders of crusades / Holy Wars and the rest.

Motion (pure movement, neuter) turned into the self-conscious (lower mind) e-motion is a necessary stage, typified in all the exoteric religions by some allegory of eating fruit off the Tree of Knowledge, the 'forbidden' fruit which carries us downwards into evolution when uncontrolled, but then helps us climb the return arc of evolution-back-to-One-ness as knowledge improves / expands and finally enables us to rein the selfish / runaway emotions so that we end up with Knowing.

Much lower forms of magic, nearly always black, i.e. selfish are done on this plane; as are ideological indoctrination, propaganda, advertising, and the like.

Prana, the Life forces of the galaxies, easily cause the *e*-motions to spurt and to flare when once the (lower) mind control has supplied the twist or the impetus.

This, too, is the plane of much negative psychism like unconscious mediumship, unconscious telepathy – and, more powerful, of unconscious 'kriyashakti' (technical term) for 'results produced on the outer planes by inner thoughts and feelings'; anything from a wart on your hand 'due to worry', to ill-effects on others due to 'ill-feelings' be these 'bad luck', curses, or whatever.

It's no use blinding ourselves by decrying 'superstitions, like the evil-eye', hoping that our uninformed scorn will banish realities of the emotional body; nor too is it any good leaving the tiresome job to some fancy saviour/ He-god whose sole purpose seems to be at our beck and call; we have to learn and understand and master the LAW; hence be able intelligently to control this emotional body;

to use its massive 'movement' to carry humanity up the evolutionary return arc to One-ness.

In fuller Knowledge.

By our own efforts.


4. *Prana* The vivifying Life forces of the galaxies, not really a separate 'body' but a flowing Principle that waters all.

*Technical names*

Now that you, the reader, have raised yourself to be a Researcher, let's get straight the technical names for the whole 'lotus' of the seven bodies.

1. Physical. Technical term = Stula sarira.
2. Health or etheric. Technical term = Linga sarira.
3. Emotions. Technical term = Kama-Manas.
4. Life Forces. A principle, i.e. Prana.

(often this Principle is placed at number two position; in fact it is everywhere.)

(And, moving on to the story of our subsequent chapters:)

5. Mind. Technical term = Manas.

Not only higher Manas (the formless) and lower Manas (the concrete mind), but also the 'bridge' between, technically known as 'ahamkara', that is, the sense of I am I.

6. Love-Wisdom. Technical term = Buddhi (from Bodh, that is, true knowledge, discriminately accurate). A general 'feeling of well-being, that is, love' is hopelessly inadequate. Discriminating Principle is an alternative name for this sixth plane, where one-ness becomes understood and meaningful Buddha-hood.

7. Truth / One-ness / Supreme. Technical term = Atma. Again not strictly 'a body', but infusing all and all-ness, both in Space and in Time / Time-less.

All the seven inter-weave, interlock, and inter-penetrate; at every level, in every way.

All seven are each 'sevenfold times seven', i.e. with at least 49 main areas / strata / degrees. Even our physical skin has seven medical layers; the fourth being the thickest / densest as the 'above' and the 'below' both overlap this fourth layer.

The whole seven form a 'lotus flower' – of ordered purpose, when complete, but lop-sided in dis-harmony when incomplete as at present because humanity is only in the fifth-sub race of the Fifth Root Race. Yet to be brought forth are:

(a) The two remaining sub-roots of this, the current, Fifth Root Race, i.e. the sixth sub-root race (as foreshadowed in North America and elsewhere; tall; tending to 'play a hunch') and the yet-unknown seventh sub-root race. These two sub-roots will jointly be the pioneers of clairvoyance, clairaudience, clairsentience – clear seeing (of sounds, of the 'invisible' / formless), clear hearing (of thoughts, Life forces, Harmony of the Spheres), and clear knowing (Truth / One-ness).

The exoterics sometimes call these three: Omniscient, Omnipresent, Omnipotent. All humanity can and should, each and every one of us, reach the 'triangular states' before the end of this manvantara (4,320,000,000 years) cycle of eternity.

(*b*) The Sixth Root Race, (not the above sixth sub-race), with its seven sub-root races. All, thousands of millenia thence; now entirely unknown in this village, planet earth, but not necessarily to Space Peoples in the multi-fold vastnesses of the galaxies.

(*c*) The Seventh Root Race (with also seven sub-root races therein) which will complete the story. The final culmination, aeons later, will flower our present cycle of eternity of manvantara by which time humanity will be truly of One-Ness/Truth.

To repeat, there is no commonsense reason at all why examples of states of conscious/powers depicted by our future root races cannot function and actually exist now, right now, outside this village, planet earth. Such conceit/fear is unworthy of humanity – or of One-ness.

The galaxy, even the local one, is a big big place with over one thousand million habitable planets or more planets than there are houses in this mud-speck village of us five-sensers.

We need to grow. Let's start now.


5. *Mind body* or *Manas*. By which is meant not only the higher Manas and the lower (concrete) Mind, but the bridge between – the differentiated consciousness, the separate 'soul' so plugged by some exoterics (how in the name of Truth can 'a soul' become separated, cut-off from the All-Soul, the Over-Soul, The Source? One-ness IS!), and called in occultism 'Ahamkara' the knowingness that has reached the (partial) state of at least knowing that 'I am I'.

Now, progress for humanity depends on which of those dual 'I's' gets the emphasis – the lower 'I' of the downward involution into matter (selfish/warlike/take rather than give) or the higher 'I' of the return evolutionary arc back to One-ness so that harmony, which is balance, which is Justice/Equilibrium, increasingly manifest. In final perfection of the Seventh Root Race both the dual 'I's' become re-absorbed in the middle 'am', that is, the first vowel, or flowing centre of initial force/impulse, and the middle consonant, that is, the centre of the 'market place'. Let's realize then, that 'am' will be sublimated to 'the

41

quality from which it comes' or to 'am-ness' – often allegoried by eastern exoteric religions as OM, or AUM, the mystic sound 'whence all proceeds', and which has to be 'pronounced in seven ways', which created in six days plus the seventh of rest / perfection, or the 'word of seven syllables'; the state where the 'mind is clear, still and reflective'; where real meditation begins.

Extremely foolish (sorry! but that word is deserved) are those who confuse this alert mind state 'clear as rock crystal' with the harmful rubbish of 'paralysing the mind / going beyond the mind' – the high road to imbalance, to ending up as an 'occult wreck', brought about by our own rash / stupid / undiscriminating – faith / belief.

Not, positively not, occult at all.

Positively harmful is the negative state of sitting passive, with your mouth wide open (even metaphorically) waiting for it to be stuffed with ambrosia from some fancy He-god / guru / deva or any other Sugar Daddy, dead or alive.

Man must progress by his own efforts; on his own two flat feet; in balance – conscious balance – knowing the why and the what of LAW; studied, applied, discriminatingly / accurately in full KNOWLEDGE. Wish-wash won't do. Misty-seeing (mystics) won't do. Intuition has, always, to be exact / true / spot-on. Always, not just often, or usually.

That's humanity's task. And it can be done – using mind. Manas.

What then is the essential quality of Manas? We all know the lower concrete mind – an Einstein, Mr Tycoon, The President / Prime Minister / Arch Bishop. We all have a touch (ambition!) of that, and know, for positive certain, that it is separate / selfish, even when camouflaged as 'doing it for the good of my country / society / religion / science', etc. It's the filthy word 'my' that gives it away!

What then is the truer wholeness-quality of higher mind? It's a state as far removed from most of us as are the Space Peoples – how do you explain to a stone the fragrance of a flower? How do you explain to the cleverest / most powerful monkey the fragrance of poetry?

42

Come to think of it, how do you explain it to an encrusted scientist – such realms being way beyond the frame-work of his proof/evaluate/analyse and his vaunted nuts-and-bolts technique is woefully inadequate. Yet he has the cheek, having totally failed with fragrance of poetry which even he knows to be, to pontificate about the vast unknowns of the galaxies, and blithely expects you (even gets huffy if you don't!) to accept what he says is 'scientific' by which he means true, or as far as truth can be known.

So, what is the vital difference between lower and higher Manas, Space-Mind? With the very very best of a lower mind, however trained, however intuitive, you still have to pick up a book, physically, to read it; you still have to grub through page by page (however fast/well you skim) to understand it. You're as stuck as that, be you professor or peasant.

Pathetic, isn't it?!

With higher Manas (technical term/state), without picking up the book, without even going into the library/country/planet (yes! planet!!), you would KNOW fully, accurately, completely:

what was in the book,

what was in the mind of the author while writing the book,

what was in *all* the minds that influenced the mind of the author while writing the book,

be those minds on this planet or not; in physical incarnation or not.

And, you would know it instantly.

By now every practical, sensible chap will have fainted. But – how do you explain fragrance to a stone, or poetry to an animal with the five-only little senses of an earthling?

These higher states, beyond the 'form', beyond the 'known', beyond this village, planet earth; can be very very different. Certainly they are not as puny and as restricted as our 'pastpresentfuture' stuck in one single rut time, for instance. And even we earthlings, of only-five senses, can get out of this time rut when freed from our dense physical bodies, for example, when we 'think' of being in some other place/time/state, or when we 'dream'.

43

True Yogis and Initiates – and there is no reason at all why all of us should not become one, with perseverence and with training, in one life or another – can and do have this faculty/attribute of the higher Manas, at conscious Will, in Knowledge.

Even the most dense of us have had an occasional flash.

Now, at last, are we in a position to understand the Powers of the Mind over Matter.

# 4. Powers of the Mind

Man, the Thinker, is the 'one free creative agent in Nature' free to be very good – very bad, on a staggering scale of the 'good' which lower-Manas cannot really envisage.

But each cause produces effect, and LAW ensures that the initiator of the effect, you, restores the balance. There can be no justice, no reason in some tame saviour doing all the dirty work for you.

But what is 'you'? It includes your four lower bodies (physical, health, desire-mind, prana energy) and your fifth – Manas, which combine to link 'you' with all things, all no-things.

This is a big point.

'You' are time-less; 'you' are space-less. It is only the four lower bodies, or tools that you seat in the chair, that are in incarnation (or not), that are 'separate' from other people, other things, other no-things. The real 'you' is the upper/inner part of your Manas, plus the two other 'bodies' we have not yet fully discussed – the Love-Wisdom Sixth of Buddhi and the Truth/One-ness Seventh of Atma. This inner triad (higher Manas, Buddhi, Atma) being in all-time (no-time), all-space (no planet) and being all-linked One-ness.

So the LAW is 'you', or rather 'you' and LAW are both of the 'same Source'. One-ness IS. Nothing is, nor can be, separate from or outside of One-ness. Obviously!

One-ness IS.

But Man, the Thinker, can distort One-ness temporarily, and can muck about with the balance of LAW as he learns to develop/exercise his free will. But, but, but:

sooner or later, in one life or another, he has to restore the balance by himself, through himself, of himself.

And, in full. To the exact scale of the distortion. It would be altogether too unjust to expect to get away with it, and to land someone else/something else with the bulk (or even a part) of the burden.

It is fortunate, because the realization of Justice, of Equilibrium soon restrains Man in the exercise of the tremendous powers of Manas. Siddhis is the technical term. True Yogis and true Intiates have always had these powers, even in this village, planet earth, although decried by the encrusted. The powers were not widely demonstrated, for weighty reasons as we shall see, but were discriminatingly used 'by the Golden Thread' of evolutionary-return arc beings like Joshua Ben Pendara (the Essene Master of Righteousness, whom the exoteric Christians confuse with Jesus, the Nazarene), Apollonius of Tyana (damned by the exoterics), Comte St Germain ('proved' a fake by the exoterics), Cagliostro (condemned and murdered by the exoterics), Mesmer (persecuted as a fraud by the exoterics who have now degraded his 'magnetic fluid' into hypnotism or the imposition of a stronger will on to a weaker), H. P. Blavatsky (denounced as a fraud/charlatan/Russian spy by the exoterics and even banished from the headquarters (paid for largely by her) of her own society when dying and when she appealed to be allowed to go there because of the warmth of the climate.) Paracelsus (he had his skull broken by assassins hired by a cardinal), and many other noble fellow-martyrs seeking to help involutionary-down-into-matter-earthlings who were smeared, persecuted and cast out by all except those of the evolutionary return arc who were beginning 'to have eyes to see'.

To say 'they knew him not' is more true than the separatists think.

SECTION 1. *The Powers, or Siddhis*

Increasingly apparent as 'you' – the true seven-bodied being, begin to use more than just nuts and bolts.

At first spasmodic; just enough to show that they exist;

next, personal – for you and yours, be it the family, the tribe, the nation, the group, the ideal – in essence 'yours', that is, selfish, or at least self-centred; hence of lower Manas. Because 'once across the bridge' (ahamkara), once 'across the stream', once 'enlightened', 'you' automatically function in higher Manas, in whole-ness – where selfishness ceases. One-ness IS.

These lower siddhis of the lower Manas are of great power, and by use of the lower Manas can be controlled the pranic Life forces magnifying the powers/state called desire-mind, plus those of the etheric. Giving results and range far beyond the present known psychokinetics, paranormal, extra-sensory, telepathic, clairvoyant powers.

Bending metal spoons by focused lower Manas, mind-reading; 're-assembling' be it to re-start broken watches/machinery or be it to apport or to materialize distant objects – all these and much more are easily done; easily understood.

But. The price has to be paid.

In full.

By the doer.

Those three inexorably are.

Nuts-and-bolts folk just do not appreciate these devastating points. After all, they argue 'quite reasonably' from their point of view: if you can do a trick and have acquired the skill, why not give repeat performance/proof? Where is the harm in a trained pianist playing every night, of a skilled surgeon doing many operations, of a scientist repeatedly testing to establish a theory? So 'reasonable' at that level.

Take the story of Jesus, of Buddha, of Zarathustra, of Osiris, or any other you like; all loved humanity, which knew them not and killed them, say the stories: – so let's consider; if Jesus was divine, and came to save, and

47

we (stupid) men failed to recognize the light; then why did he not re-incarnate every Thursday till we finally cottoned on? As the son of god, presumably he could. If he loved us, then why not continue till we clots learnt?

Because of the price that had to be paid – including by 'you', the seven-bodied being of One-ness, of Law. More harm than good would result to 'you' and to humanity, by re-incarnating every Thursday. It goes like this.

The sevenfold 'you' is the One free agent in Nature and is linked in your seven bodies with All and All-ness, so that the result of 'your' actions are enormous; and are charged directly to you, for good or ill; be you 'aware' of it, or be you argumentative nuts-and-bolts. After all, gamma rays still have their effect whether the powerful jungle-chief agrees on their existence or not. Whether the monkey realizes the fragrance of poetry, or not, such fragrance (and much much more) is.

When an evolutionary-arc being (Jesus, Buddha, St Germain, Mesmer or Blavatsky) comes into contact with earthlings, the whole sevenfold aura of 'you' is activated: let us suppose that 'you' are half good, half bad, as are so many of us multi-millions at the bottom of the involutionary arc and struggling to get round the turning point to go back up the return arc of evolution.

Contact with such a superior being causes far more than 'normal' disturbance of our aura and the good is activated to heights beyond us 'unaided'. And that is fine. But, what of the bad? Look at the stupid things we all tend to do when in a blind temper or blind drunk; they are as nothing compared to the aura activation now being discussed where the lower mind, Manas, connects us with vast ranges far, far beyond our normal span of physical effects; plus our Prana (Life forces) that spurt/flare when unchecked; plus our emotions (Kama-Manas or Desire-Mind); plus our etheric – all giving a scope to the 'bad' beyond our wildest imaginations – a scope beyond space/time, beyond this village, planet earth, beyond earthlings/animals/birds/plants, a scope stretching out/in to All.

And every single iota of 'bad' is chargeable, directly, solely, to 'you'/'us'.

No wonder the 'Golden Thread' of evolutionary arc Beings, and the Space Peoples, choose their contacts with great, great care. All too easy would be the activation of more bad than of good.

But, But, But!

As humanity in its millions is now of the fifth sub-race of the Fifth Root Race and is therefore past the half-way stage of the turning point;

and as increasingly there is more good than there is bad in 'you'/'us';

so too increasingly are the opportunities for mostly-beneficial aura activation.

But. But. But!

The cautious discriminating approach is as essential as ever. The 'Golden Thread' Beings always focused earthling attention on the need for discrimination; do not all the stories of Them show that they did miracles, enacted cures, gave signs, produced wonders only and solely on limited occasions and in chosen times. Jesus did not heal all, for instance; he used to select, and with good reason.

So too today. The Space Peoples make contact with very great care – 'we don't choose you, you choose us' or if we have got ourselves round the turning point, back on to the return upward arc sufficiently (and by our own efforts) to be able to sustain a contact, or to have more good than bad results in an activated aura.

As a humanity in Western Culture we are now being sparingly and carefully and gradually shown powers of the mind over matter – be it over metal/over waters/ over thoughts – as parapsychology retreats in the face of advancing para-knowledge, that is, of the Occult sciences. Uri Geller is well known; so too are increasing numbers of others. Let us remember that governments have invested huge sums of money to investigate – the Russian, the American, the British; in that chronological order; with the Americans currently spending most, and having overtaken the Russian lead.

As a Uri Geller, or his equivalent, demonstrates, and as we earthlings argue that it's a trick/fake/genuine we all activate our auras – not over much we hope – and

49

learn to expand/cope. The glorious factor about TV is that millions of us can simultaneously take part and therefore directly experience the single studio event; in the old days the Being had to wander the face of the earth physically affecting isolated groups; now One-ness IS becomes more instant.

In Eastern Cultures with the more advanced metaphysical mind (page 43) the earthlings have long been able to understand and to use Occult powers, and now finally, slowly, reluctantly are convincing the West.

All because of the comprehension that 'you' are not just a physical body,

are not merely triple,

but are sevenfold.

So let us now realize more deeply how these powers of the mind-over-matter work, and why repeated experiments are not as 'reasonable' a request as was superficially first thought.

SECTION 2. *Examples of Power of Mind*

*Telepathy* is perhaps the most common and most famous of such Siddhis, or inner Powers. Where is the mother who has not 'known' what her child needed – in a manner beyond the normal five senses? Where is the group that have not 'heard' of such instances, throughout the cultures, throughout the centuries?

Even the Royal College of (Materialistic) Science has stopped talking about 'electrical discharge impulses from the brain'. As long ago as the 1960s an experiment was done jointly by Cambridge University of England, by an American University, near Chicago, and by Leningrad University in USSR, done at Leningrad, where the transmitter telepath was seated in a lead-box of a sufficient insulation to keep out any known cosmic/electrical/gamma rays; and then, in addition, the lead-box with the transmitter telepath inside was immersed – totally – in a bath of mercury (think of the expense of all this!); yet the transmitter telepath was able to transmit thoughts which the receiver telepath outside wrote down accurately; instantly.

Accurately, instantly are the key words. Negative telepathy, where impulses/thoughts were received by you 'did not quite know how' have long been familiar. In the 1914–18 war the European powers had large numbers of African troops on war duty abroad, and repeated are the stories of the White administrators in Africa being approached by natives who wanted leave to go home to their villages because 'their brother abroad on war service had just been wounded or lost a limb or died in action'. In those days the war dispatches took several days, yet the natives knew instantly, and abundantly were proved right. The British, the French the German, the Portuguese, the Belgian administrators, all reported/recorded/documented these repeated proofs over the four years of the war.

But, they did not know *how* they knew.

Now motive is everything, in true Occultism. What do you think would happen to a man who proved, beyond all doubt, that he could always, accurately instantly read thoughts? All thoughts. Very soon his government would realize that he could read the thoughts – accurately, instantly – of the 'enemy government'. Then what would happen to the poor chap? It would not take long to realize, too, that not only could he read the enemy thoughts and transmit them to his government, but that he could equally do the reverse and send the top secret stuff straight over to the enemy. What then would happen to the poor chap? It would be little use banishing him to St Helena, because he could still read/ transmit from there.

What then would happen to the poor chap?

Motive is everything, in true Occultism. Selfless-ness. One-ness.

However, some general guide-lines are known:
telepathy is positively not physical, not electrical impulses/rays or anything as dense as that. Hence it is totally beyond the range of materialistic science which focuses uniquely on the outermost of the seven bodies, on the outer form;

understanding has to approach inwards:

first, to the etheric. Here are most of the instances of negative psychism, such as the African examples above, of people 'knowing' their own very-near – in anguish / death on the one hand or in joy / exultation on the other, that is, in the extremes of stimulation, be it bad / good end of the spectrum.

But such people seldom know 'how'; such people often are uncluttered, simple or primitive, the type all of us earthlings used to be before 'The Fall' (page 21), before spirit was overcome by matter, before the central eye was closed / replaced by the dual eyes towards the end of Lemuria and the middle of Atlantis; or at least, when the third sub-root (we're the fifth sub-root) of our Fifth Root Race of the Chaldees, and their magic. Anyway, of long ago.

More understanding further inwards from the etheric, to the Prana (life forces), into the desire-mind body of Kama-Manas and increasingly two factors emerge:

(1) your telepathy gets more powerful, far-ranging and accurate, (2) you learn to control it, understand it, and can switch it on or off – at will.

And if your motive is less than Whole-ness; is personal / mercenary / separative; then the greater the power – the greater the kick-back. Woe to the selfish so-called occultist.

Let's take an example of 'Manas-telepathy', i.e. done by $A$ in knowledge and by will on $B$, who is readily co-operating and knows what is going on:

$B$'s etheric / prana / kama-manas would expand; their stretch under this activation of aura would include most of the life, say as far as the moon; all life (mineral, vegetable, animal, human) including the 'lives' of the 'elemental essences' (technical term) that activate the auras of all within range;

not only the good-bad in $B$ would be thrown-out-into-result, but that of the wholeness at those levels and as far away as the moon. Please think. Please consider the consequences.

Would you lightly 'demonstrate telephathy'? Would

you undertake repeated experiments? Repeatedly activating all that with all those results, all charged to you!

And that was of *B* readily co-operating and knowing what was happening – of *B* having an aura more good than bad – of *B* helping to control.

Please please think what price would be paid for indiscrimate use on *B, C,D*, etc., to *Z*, when they did not know/were not co-operating, and suddenly had their auras activated throwing-out-into-result what was within, even if more bad than good.

No wonder the 'Golden Thread' of Osiris, Buddha, Jesus, Mesmer, Blavatsky all stressed discrimination, and cured/healed only when 'allowable under LAW'. No wonder the Space Peoples make contact cautiously with earthlings.

We all have much to learn. Let's start now.


SECTION 3. *The Principle behind these Siddhis (Powers)* is One-ness.

By the power of Manas, Mind, 'you' cease as a physical separate and become as a One-ness in X, the object/siddhi.

To do that means 'gathering two or three together so that I am' or gathering the physical + etheric + Kama-manas + prana bodies together so that One-ness 'am', that is, the source energy of the first vowel A + the middle consonant M of the alphabet, focused in the 'market place' which then was the centre of temporal activity, i.e. focused in the mid-point, i.e. the all-point/no-point so that All is possible/manifested.


SECTION 4. *Examples of Other Siddhis (Powers)*
affect metals, plants, animals.
    liquids, air, weather.
    thoughts, feelings, actions.
make things:

big or small
appear or disappear
move from here to there
travel in space
materialize – dematerialize
instantaneous Space Travel, not the grubbing around
with light years
be in more than one place at a time
move in time
forward or back
pre-cognition    post-cognition
and so much more.

All of us, in one life or another, will do all these – and
more. One-ness IS.

Many an earthling – particularly in the metaphysical
East – can do most/all these now. Many many many
Space Peoples can do all/more now.

How about you? Are you stuck – or are you 'moving
along the way'? It's your choice, your responsibility, your
destiny. But it is a choice, and it has to be made; sooner
or later.


SECTION 5. *The Principle Applied* – Smile

Let's suppose you had never smiled, never known it,
no one around you could understand/demonstrate the
faculty of smile.

After all, that was recently Western peoples' experience/
attitude to Extra-Sensory powers of mind over metal.

How then would you at-one with smile?

You might first of all be 'scientific' and with your nuts-
and-bolts gravely measure the opening of the face, note
that smile 'only' happened there, get the average mean
duration (repeatedly checked) of Brown/White/Black/
Yellow faces, of old/young and the rest of that other stuff.
Terribly correct.

And what would be your solemn conclusion, arrived at
by huge cross-checking consensus?

That a smile was an opening, a contraction of the
muscles of the face.

Because that is as far as outer-only form, dense physical only body, modern science can go. Woefully inadequate.

Now how did you 'know' smile? Warm smile, sad / happy / weak / strong / deceitful / beautiful – how did you 'know'?

By becoming at-one 'you' yourself became warm / sad / happy, etc.

Then you 'realized' that smile was not only on the lips – it could be 'felt' at the back of the head; further, that you could see through the back of your own head to feel the smile. Further, that having become warm once, years ago, you were / are warm now. In all those intervening years the warmth of your smile had not got cold, and instantly 'warm smile' was available.

You *know* this to be true.

How would you have explained it to a nuts-and-bolts scientist who had never (wanted to) realize the quality of smile?

Ask him where the smile 'goes to' when it's not wrapped round the face. How far away? How fast does it travel back?

Faster than the speed of light? Because the nuts-and-bolts say there *can't* be anything faster!

How is it that the smile, the same smile?, can appear on several faces at once – on a huge crowd, at once. How many smiles had to be fetched, from where? how fast? to brighten all those faces watching a TV coast-to-coast hook-up.

Will we run out of smile? Use it all up? Like the nuts-and-bolts say we shall for the energy of the solar system. Is smile an energy? Usable up? Do you run out of it when you're thirty-five, sixty, ninety years old?

*See* how woefully inadequate are nuts-and-bolts when dealing with
Smile.    At-one.    Occult.    Truth.


SECTION 6. *The Chakras, the force centres*
An additional main clue to the understanding of the faculty of smile, or to any other application of the

55

principle of One-ness, hence of the use of the Powers of the Mind is to 'bring into Life' the centres in the bodies relevant to each power or force – these are the Chakras.

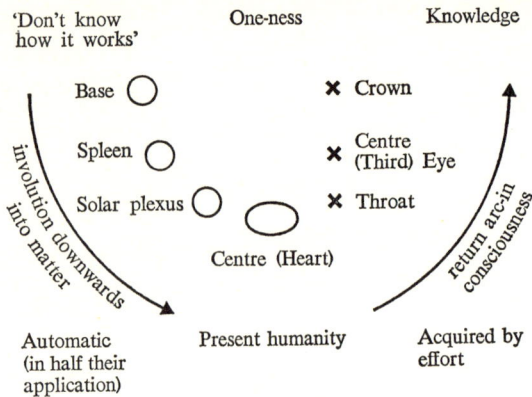

| 'Don't know how it works' | One-ness | Knowledge |
|---|---|---|
| Base ◯ | | ✘ Crown |
| Spleen ◯ | | ✘ Centre (Third) Eye |
| Solar plexus ◯ | ◯ | ✘ Throat |
| | Centre (Heart) | |

*involution downwards into matter* — *return arc in consciousness*

| Automatic (in half their application) | Present humanity | Acquired by effort |
|---|---|---|

As is usual in this current earthling time span, or Manvantara (technical term) of 4,320,000,000 years, the Chakras too are sevenfold, as are the Root Races, the Bodies, and their Senses; each 7 being divided by 7, and yet again by 7, to state only the broad outlines.

In times past, earthlings over those millions and millions of years have developed the first three Chakras – base, spleen, solar plexus – and these now function 'automatically', without effort. For instant, where is the man who can't get into a temper? We're all experts at that, it comes 'naturally'.

Producing a serene, calm, fully reflective mind is not yet automatic and requires distinct practice, effort and perseverence, and the Siddhis (or powers) of the mind become operative increasingly after this stage, to a vastness, to a dazzling upliftment only dimly foreshadowed by section 4. The scope and the hope for Man is breath-takingly glorious; many are those already well on the way, all others can start. Now.

All the exoteric religions refer to the Chakras, of course; the Christian calls them the 144,000 who shall be saved. Ridiculous are those who drag that down to a nuts-and-bolts level and a far truer insight may be gained from a study as below:

56

| | | | |
|---|---|---|---|
| 1. Base | 4 petals | | |
| 2. Spleen | 6 petals | | |
| 3. Solar Plexus | 10 petals | | |
| 4. Centre ('Heart') | 12 petals | | |
| 5. Throat | 16 petals | 48 'increase' to | |
| | | 96 which is | |
| | — | — | |
| 6. Centre (Third) Eye | 48+48 | 144 | |
| 7. Crown 'multiply' x 1,000 = 144,000 | | | |

So we notice that the first five stages are simple addition of petals. We start with the four of the base Chakra; perhaps the four corners of the (physical) world from which we shall be gathered together (the square of a Freemason, the cube of a Moslem, the solid of Plato, etc.), for example, the four elements of fire, air, water and earth.

At about the halfway stage, the fifth, of these, 20 petals below/18 above, we come to the (Lower) Centre Chakra, which the Christians have degraded into 'Heart' as they have densified 'Love' into syrup – Harmony, Balance, Justice, Truth being nearer the original Gnostic reality – and this (lower) Centre Chakra had better be redefined, therefore: a 7-fold Vital centre, 'double-spaced', at the mid-point between Crown and Base, where the dual forces are activated (the centripetal and the centrifugal) to flow 'downwards/outwards' to duality and 'upwards/inwards' to unification in the 2 lobed Third Eye (Centre, higher). It is at this mid-point that the Lipika Webs (technical term, for 'all' that sub-stands substance) are touched, so that Reality/One-ness actualizes. True Meditation being the first key. An entirely active process, with positively zero reliance on any one/thing/being outside.

Hence the first clue: 'double-spaced'. Many layers of meanings, of course, but an obvious one is that only 'half' of the base + spleen + solar plexus + (lower) Centre Chakras are activated – the 'half' that is automatic, or is 'without action' to use a technical term; to get them 'with action' requires the activation of the corresponding Chakra on the upward-return arc of evolution to One-ness in Knowledge (see diagram) and thus will sublimation be made reality – as willpowers of the mind be manifest.

A second clue is 'mid-point', which means that the centripetal and the centrifugal forces can both/each be made to 'flow', i.e. be activated, when the Lipika Webs are here touched/sensed/reached, where One-ness IS, where the pure, inherent, motion/throb/beat of the universe can be tapped. Once tapped how will these two forces be guided? Up/down, within/out? That decision is not, it seems, taken at this Centre (lower) but at the Centre (Third) Eye – for good – or at the lower-three Chakras – for bad, depending on the total state of the aura of the man.

The solar plexus, the power house, gives the energy to the motion, which is tapped at the (lower) 7-fold vital Centre, the so-called 'Heart', but woe to the pseudo-occultist who tries to tap the universal energy 'too low down' at the solar plexus, such premature rashness being certain to meet the point of the dagger as the cable tow is unadjusted and as the neophyte rushes forward.

And an infallible clue to know if you are forcing 'too low down'? Your motive. Is it of Wholeness/Impersonal – or separative. Sure? Please think deeper because it is so so easy to fool ourselves. For instance, if the forcing were being done 'for the sake of' – then we are merely extending the personal to include a group, and hence to exclude another group. And that motive is not of Wholeness. In the context of this book, for example 'for the sake of occultism' – as separate from science or from religion would be 'too low' – all must be in Wholeness: the nuts-and-bolts scientist (bless him) must also grow in consciousness, and the religious – adherent of a particular He-god (let's hope he blesses the occultist!) is likewise One.

Forced meditation; unprepared raising of Kundalini Fire (technical term for the energy coiled at the base Chakram); sitting for development of immature clairvoyance – all such imprudence are well known; as are the occult wrecks that ensue.

Far far wiser would be a focus on the next stage, that of the throat where animal-man links with Initiate-man, the Halo-saint, where the body gives way to the head, where the Word is sounded – in its lower echelons – and where the selfless inner powers begin, of mind, of Manas. The fifth stage.

The stage of the bridge, between the upper and the lower, between the known and the unknown, between the permament and the evanascent (page 41).

Mounting up the Chakras we notice that simple addition of petals now undergoes a change/enlargement. The total of the simple additon had come to 48 (4+6+ 10+12+16) and the '2 lobed' Chakram of the Centre (Third) Eye assimilates all the 48 on one side/lobe as the 'male' faculties 'with action'; and simultaneously on the other side/lobe as the 'female' attributes 'without action'; to give itself 96 petals (48+48). So that we have (1) a summation, a synthesis, a wholeness, in which all the 48 former petals have been transformed, (2) have become doubled/increased, and (3) have been 'absorbed' – three stages of a trinity – so that 48 has 'become' 48/48 on the visible side/lobe and a corresponding (or double-spaced) reflection in the invisible noumenon side/lobe. So that the trinity consists of two obvious/tangible 48+48 and the third 'ghost-like' resurrection/enlightenment of 'that to which they have become One', that is, '96'.

Now let us realize '96', that is, a nine and a six: nine is the occult number of self-initiation (get up on your own two flat feet and walk; and get up to the mountain top of spirit, leaving the vale of matter; by your own efforts), and the '6', the sixth state: of Love-Wisdom, of Chrestos-consciousness of the Sixth Root Race (page 41), of a stage yet more enlightened than that of Full Manas (whole mind) where the vast powers on page 53 are but the outer manifestation.

Simple addition of petals is even less applicable at the last – the seventh stage of the Crown Chakram. Taking first, 'gathered together' all the 48 petals of the physical, temporal, market-place and absorbing them 'at the top'; next taking the nine-six 'state' achieved already (Chrestos) when these 48 had been increased/enlightened; we 'add' these, conjoin these in stability, to reach a new state called 144 and then 'multiply' (by the vast inner process) – 'to increase at an enormously greater/higher/spiritual way' – to end up as the 144,000. The Crown Chakram having 'a thousand petals' of its 'own'. Thus, we are 'saved' – by our unique efforts – as we are One with One-ness.

Is this concept not more beautiful? More true? More 'uplifting'? Does it not offer a great future for Man?

Let us also look at some of the spin-offs that manifest as we mount the Chakras.

*Vegetarianism*

Let's take *vegetarianism*.

At the lower scale of the involution down into matter, the automatic or animalistic stage, we absorb food only through the hole in the face (mouth) and have, are compelled, to eliminate only through the dual holes at the other end. A bit of absorbing sunshine through the eyes/pores, and a fraction of cleansing through sweat – and that's about it.

Such is the level of 'proteins or you'll be ill', of calories, carbohydrates – and the rest of the dense down-into-matter-arc.

That's the stage where vegetarians are considered cranks, where occult is unproved – or of devil, where nuts-and-bolts flourish.

But humanity is past the lowest point of the downward arc in this fifth sub-race of the Fifth Root Race, and is turning in its millions to the upward return arc of Selflessness; some individuals are well on the way – Socrates, Leonardo da Vinci – and were vegetarians as long ago as that; millions of us are now groping to 'Health Foods' 'compost grown Natural Foods' Why?

As the higher Chakras open-in-mature-truth they really/genuinely do take Prana (life forces) from the air. Not just absorb sunshine on the beach; but regularly and at all times/weathers. We cease to want solid dense animalistic foods stuffed into the hole in our face – we are truthfully absorbing sufficient life forces from the Chakras – and begin to resent:

1. the high meats (relics of Atlantis, see page 23)

2. blood meats (as we switch to chicken/fish)

3. next to vegetarianism, when we enter a new cycle as we progress along the return upward arc:

(a) vegetables, etc., are staple diet. In the early stages of this we babble about our tummy, about how much better we feel, how much healthier we are, etc., etc.

(b) lifting the focus off our tummy, and its fads, we start talking about cruelty to animals, about not murder/cut up into pieces to feed the hole-in-the-face

(c) we cease to talk/preach, and become vegans (no dairy produce, e.g. milk – got by deliberate cruelty of over-fattening the cow; eggs, i.e. killing incipient life, etc.) But unless yet higher Chakras have truly opened we shall fool ourselves by pretending we're 'advanced', we'll fall ill, lack iron/calcium in our blood, and it will serve us right

(d) fruit replaces vegetables, as the main diet. The word 'spiritual' becomes meaningful. For most of us that is millenia off, sub-root races hence

(e) Prana supplies all – Elimination is ceased. The hole-in-the-face is better absorbed 'sounding the word'. The dual holes at the other end are closed, the orifices are guarded, the lodge is tiled.

Why then do we expect all Space Peoples to have a hole-in-the-face? Why should they necessarily be at such a low level of the downward into matter arc – where wars are, selfishness is.


*Other Spin-offs*

With the (true) opening of the higher Chakras come as we increasingly link in One-ness, and as the powers of section 4 manifest.

The reader will have noticed that these are very sparingly outlined, and might be irritated at such; the studious researcher will have long since realized the all-important point of right motive, and will wonder if wisdom should detail the way to these powers, perhaps used for less than Wholeness/impersonal motives; the deeply thoughtful will already be along the way to acquiring them.

Let's hope the next section helps us all.

The first four chapters are done; the first steps have been taken, the first four corners have been gathered together.

It's time to grow. Let's start now.

# PART TWO
# *YOGA*

## 5. Essential

Yoga is a science. Yoga is an art-mode of inner-sound.
Yoga is Life. Yoga is operative occultism in Magic,
true magic.

It is as old as the hills, literally. He who truly can
comprehend it in depth has the freedom of a solar system,
literally. The fact that Western Culture would not believe
it, alters nothing of Truth.

As deep, and far deeper, than the science of the West
– its laws are as exact, and have to be mastered in as many
details. As beautiful, and far more wide-reaching as the
glorious symphonies of the West, it is infinitely more
difficult to 'compose' or operate – but is stupendous in its
outer and inmost results when done in space and not, in
time and not.

Yet, all mankind has the power, has the destiny, to
master yoga – in one life or another.

Let's start now.


Section 1. *Conventional Yoga*

There is no such thing, of course. At first the
Western Cultures tended to despise it, and some foolish
ones still do; then they began to investigate, very gingerly;

a spate of books followed over the years, that went
something like this:

63

Yoga was started/done by Patanjali. A bloke. Much argument as to the date finally revealed that Patanjali was a generic name spanning mellennia upon millennia; some 5000 B.C. according to nuts-and-bolts, some 5000 millennia B.C. According to deeper students.

Yoga was breathing exercises, standing on your head, a trance – you ended up (hopefully!) more beautiful and healthy.

Yoga gave you powers – you could levitate/disappear/read thoughts; you could also make plants grow, cure ills. You sorta kinda were handy to have at call.

So people set out to acquire/grab/take these powers.

The next generation of books deliberated over the various kinds of yoga and, again, went something like this:

Yoga is of seven kinds: Raja the kingly, the Royal Yoga embracing—
Jnana, or Knowledge yoga (said to be suitable for Western nuts-and-bolts brains);
Bhakti yoga – devotional, just love/syrup/emotionalize along; invariably with some guru, deva, He-god, etc.
Karma yoga – work/drudgery – simply grin and bear it sweat, and trust the 'next life' you'll do better.

Understandably, some people got impatient with that, and wanted quick results. Instant yoga. 'Practical' Yoga that would smite the enemy/fill the honey pots/bring results (tangible, visible) – now!

So came Mantra Yoga – of chants, of rituals, of rosary beads, of repetitive prayers/sutras/invocations.

Also Laya yoga – of intense (lower) focus – be it on your own navel and hence of electroplasmic power, or be it on the pin you stuck in the enemy effigy, or on the gold you craved. All camouflaged, of course, under incense, soaring music, fancy clothes/fancy places, Cathedrals/Mosques/Temples – as was Mantra yoga.

Lastly the well-known Hatha Yoga, of the body.
Anything from physical exercise to live longer/better.

A bit of breathing through the right and the left nostril. And that was it.

Oh yes, there were, of course, the Thou shalt – Thou

shall not rules/commandments/observances/Nidana
(knots that tangled you in matter), etc.

Oh, and the postures – the Asanas – as you lay on your
back/sat in the Lotus posture/balanced on one finger
(literally), and thought thoughts of Brahma, the Boss
Deva/God/Supreme.

If actually you were 'in' then you said Samadhi as well.
And that was that.
Yoga, westernized.


SECTION 2. *A better approach to Yoga*

Might it not be a better idea to follow the guiding
threads, a bit tangled (purposely) of the man who seemed
to know more about it – the Gautama Buddha, perhaps
the finest flowering of earthling humanity as yet.

Of course, it is even more tangled (purposely) to follow
the outer threads; the phenomenon (instead of the
noumenon), the visible (instead of the inner invisible),
the temporary and the evanascent.

How are we going to seek with the inner ear, the inner
eye? How are we going to 'merge thy senses into one
sense, that sense alone which lies concealed in the hollow
of thy brain'? Shall we start with the Great Architect of
the Universe – arithmetic, then try the Grand
Geometrician – Concentric Key (eh! what's that? Please
see much below); before fluffing out our auras to the Most
High – Truth.

Let's take Wheels. Fifteen Wheels. Why 15? Well the
7 visible + the 7 invisible plus the synthesis; the 7 above
+ the 7 below, 7 matter + 7 spirit, and so on.

Or the 15 of the full Manas; the five of the concrete
brain and its five senses, the five of the bridge, ahamkara,
'I am I' consciousness (page 41), and the five of the
metaphysical mind to give the full Manas of page 42.

After all, Manas is probably the best tool we've got,
and we do all have some.

So let's take a deep slow breath, controlled and
counted, like good Pranayama yogis and – continue.

SECTION 3. *The Principles*

Moderation; perseverance; discrimination will unfold step by regulated step the inner veils of Nature as we become conscious co-workers with her.

With – is the operative word. Any hint of separation, any thought even, and disaster in related degree is inevitable. Yes, that harsh word – inevitable.

So the dangers are clear. No one has any excuse of ignorance. Yet the prizes of yoga are so great that many have sought them 'too low down', not in wholeness, but in personalized separation and have suffered the inexorable consequences in one life or another.

The second reality of yoga is that none can teach you, but yourself. It simply is not of Truth to have to rely on stimuli from outside, on guidance from without – be it from a school, a book, a teacher, a deva inspiration, a thought-form that some call god.

The path has, absolutely has; to be forged, not merely followed; alone – quite alone; by the seeker.

European parsons and scientists both revolt at this. The former has been conditioned to rely on his external 'holy' book and his (separated off) god; the scientist has long been accustomed to obeying his system (called science) with its miniscule framework of reference that focuses solely on the outer form and leaves outside the terms of its study the vast flowing streams of multi-faceted Life.

No wonder they both look askance at yoga, which has no path – you have to make it

relies solely on oneself

insists, begs, and demands – total, but total, unselfishness of motive.

And punishes failure with due effects lasting many lives.

Yet the prizes are enormous.

What happens to a Teacher, willing to 'teach yoga', or to an author writing a book on it, a book that anyone can obtain, be he 'ready' or not? The price has to be paid, in full, of the errors made by the pupil or by the reader where the actions have been so activated.

66

A very very sobering fact. Of course, a due proportion of the good results are also gleaned by the activators – so hope remains.

However, it becomes easy to understand why there is no (genuine) exoteric teaching either written or spoken; why all is veiled in allegory, as the seeker dissolves the veils in ordered progression, as he himself advances; why broad principles alone are freely stated, such as those given by the Gautama Buddha, below.


SECTION 4. *The Eightfold Path*

RIGHT: views, intention, speech, action, livelihood, effort, mindfulness, concentration.

That bald statement of the Noble Eightfold path is so well known as almost to be a platitude. So what has it to do with yoga?

Page 63 said Yoga is a science; is an art-mode of inner speech, and likened it to a glorious symphony of Life. Well, how do you write a symphony? What are the rules? You can take most reasonably bright men, teach them the trade, and they will make serviceable bridges across rivers, or power stations that give electric light. But how do you design a school for producing symphonies? Clear-cut definite / regular / tested rules of the nuts-and-bolts wobble and waver when faced with the flow of Life, such as great and timeless symphonies are; as is yoga.

Yet the laws may not be transgressed. Discords are not the object.

The neophyte will surely seek the deepest, most inmost note – his own unique note – the occult sound to use a technical term. To reach such he must go beyond the obvious / visible / apparent to the Reality within. And how to do it?

Why not concentrate on the Chakras (see pages 55–62), the interior centres of force that manifest outer results in Law, when focused by inner / deep Thought. Right Thought.

So let us endeavour using the aids so far outlined: perseverance as we go, life after life;

moderation – in speed, in aim, in balance;
discrimination – always, at every level, *always*!
'aiming' our inner Thought at – Chakras.

Using, in the first stage, arithmetic, the Great Architect of the Universe (page 65).

And the method of movement? Wheels. Fifteen of them.

The seven orthodox forms of yoga readily can be seen to 'correspond' to the seven main Chakras:

| | |
|---|---|
| Raja | 1,000 Crown |
| Jnana<br>Bhakti | 96 Centre (Eye) |
| Karma | 16 petal, Throat<br>12 petal Centre (lower) |
| Laya | 10 petal, solar plexus |
| Mantra | 6 petal, spleen |
| Hatha | 4 petal, base |

But the correspondence is only rough and ready; so much overlap as in the more subtle qualities of Life, say as depicted by colours. When does a colour 'blue' cease to be blue and become 'green'? In which light, at which angle, with what material?

Also, to use arithmetic, the $1+2+4$ rhythm of the orthodox yoga is 'different' from the $1+1$; 2; 3 rhythm of the Chakras where we saw on page 59 how altered were the results of simple addition from (*a*) 'to increase' when the total of 48 petals, (not even 50) jumped past the 'hundred', that is, an altogether higher state of consciousness, up nearly to the one-hundred-and-fifty, that is, to 144, (*b*) when the second enormous shift 'to multiply' left even the vast expansion of 'increase' behind as it soared to the un-imaginable 'Heights' of 144,000, as it rose from Chrestos to Father – to use those Christian technical terms.

Since we know that the difference between a great symphony and hack-music is not merely that the symphony may have more notes – 144,000 but has better composition – so we must look for deeper relationships between the Chakras and their petals on the one hand; the jumps in consciousness, on the other; and of the total outpouring of the inter-blending.

To help you, dear reader, let us also consider the four spoked 'First Wheel', noting its relation to the four petals of the base Chakram and to the physical four square Hatha yoga. From being the basic note, its link to the Eightfold Noble Path is obvious, as is its further relationship to the '32 marks of Buddhahood'. We can, for the moment, consider the four spokes, the union up and down; the Jacob's 'ladder' of the Christians; but we must note 'that all four spokes do not go up or down 'at the same speed', although a 'balance' has to be achieved finally. For instance, on the way up we could progress by 'increase' and spurt metaphorically at the rate of 48 to 144; or (more hard) we could expand our consciousness at the speed of 'multiply' as we zoom from 144 to 144,000 metaphorically.

Dear reader, please persevere as we examine the Four Noble Truths.


Section 5. *The Four Noble Truths*

As we detail them, perhaps it would be possible mentally to link them to specific Chakras, to states of consciousness depicted by the seven bodies of man (physical, etheric, desire-mind, life forces, Mind, Love-Wisdom, Supreme):

1. Now this is the noble truth of pain: birth is painful, old age is painful, sickness is painful, death is painful, sorrow, lamentation, dejection and despair are painful. Contact with unpleasant things is painful, not getting what one wishes is painful.

(Each truth above depicts negative-yoga where the Chakras are unbalanced/wrong speed/ill formed. Gradually the 'number of petals worked' increases, as slowly we rise higher. If the petals were working in proper link/relation/way the reverse of pain/sorrow would BE. Genuine correction will not, repeat not, come through palliatives drawn from below-up, for example, improved breathing, better diet, more exercise, etc., but by removal of the central cause of pain / sorrow, that is, the motive – which can truly be right only 'higher up'.)

2. Now this is the noble truth of the cause of pain: that craving, which leads to rebirth, combined with pleasure and lust, finding pleasure here and there, namely the craving for passion, the craving for existence, the craving for non-existence.

(It should be remembered that, while in physical incarnation and while making full use of his physical body, the Gautama Buddha had so interlinked / interactivated his Chakras that none of the above negatives applied; in plain fact, the contrary of yoga – positive / balanced yoga – was functioning – fully. Hence too the powers of his inner bodies, as clearly he demonstrated – see / hear / touch, etc., at great distances / great sensitivity; read all thoughts; foresee time / travel back in time; and so on and on. We too, each single earthling of us, can do this far, quite easily / quite quickly. But woe if we do so 'too low down'; with motive that is not RIGHT.)

3. Now this is the noble truth of the cessation of pain: the cessation without a remainder of that craving, abandonment, forsaking, release, non-attachment.

(Not, definitely not, a shrug of the shoulders, a sort of sour-grape don't care; but a truthful let-go, an operational change in Chakra speed / level / colour which follows actually when the central motive is RIGHT, is known rightly and inwardly and truly to be *right*; exactly, accurately, throughout the levels.)

4. Now this is the noble truth that leads to the cessation of pain: this is the Noble Eightfold path, namely right views, right intention, right speech, right action, right livelihood, right effort, right mindfulness, right concentration.

(All flows from the last – right concentration, that is, right aim for the Chakras at the right levels with the right results in right balance.)

Our First Wheel had four spokes; the first wheel (or 'aim') looked to the eight points of the compass of eternity / space and of those eight took the cardinal four;

linked to the four petals of the base Chakram, because we must start yoga from where we are. The four 'spokes' having different speeds up/down as already depicted, but also different levels/ranges/subtleties/etc.; all needing right concentration, and their sequential results following in Law.

Such Right concentration would open Raja Yoga; which embraces all – witness the eight petals, the full eight points of space/time, of the Noble Eightfold 'path' 'wheels' 'aim' 'power'.)

*General comments*

Obviously the level of consciousness has been raised in four steps;

each step has different qualities or attributes in it;
each 'rises' and ranges further;
each works at a different colour/sound/light/odour/hear as its speed/aim changes with Law, activated by the central core of RIGHT motive – right concentration.

All neophytes must find their own unique occult sound – in the full vastness of its depth/scope – cleansing as they seek (see below, please).

*Suggested 'wheels' or ways to effort*

To write these in full is neither practical nor prudent. The earnest researcher should study – at first with us, if he likes, using the books suggested at the end.

The main guides as already said are (1) arithmetic.

e.g. *Wheel 2* 'starts in the full moon of July', i.e. in the seventh month; at the highest/purest of the moon – silver, i.e. pure emotion cleansed as far as pure motion – the throb of the universe, i.e. to use a technical term, at the Lipika Webs (That which sub-stands substance, i.e. all veils of manifestation).

Wheel 2 has the rhythm of 6. (The Sixth Body/Plane) Love-Wisdom 'multiplied' (in the inner sense we have already depicted) by 1,000.

The Wheel 2 has already reached inwards to a breath-taking level.

It is here that 'the hair is cut', for example, the exoteric

71

stories of Sampson and Delila, and also in other exoteric religions.

Any Grand Master, Rosecroix, Hierophant who holds his lodge / degree / stage in genuine true-magic would at this point have his hair 'standing out' – not bolt upright in fright, or with electric shock – but in response to inner powers as the petals of the sources of power began to colour. Rosenkreutz could do it with his liquid-vital, expressed in true magic of ceremonial, Mesmer could do it with his magnetic-fluid which he used for healing and for painless (major) surgical operations without anaesthetics, and H. P. Blavatsky could do it with her dhatu for the production of phenomenal magic. In the mystery schools of Samothrace it was known; in the true (hidden) occult states it still is.

It is here that the 'aim' is to face the 'East', to quote Freemasons, and others. But geography is not meant of course; which is the East of a sphere? Spherical being the shape of consciousness, of Chakras, etc.

It is here that levitation becomes easy as the Son rises to his Father, to quote the Christians.

It is during the later third-part of this wheel that the 6 x 1,000 rhythm has to be changed, under Law, to (*a*) a five-fold rhythm plus (*b*) 10 times 1,000 'transmutation to gold from silver'.

Alchemy starts too.

*Elimination*

Let us elaborate, by way of illustration, the last phrase of the previous section 'cleansing as they seek'. It means not 'just' good thoughts but these being so real and so controlled as to have direct physical results; provable, for all to see – as in the physical case of body elimination.

When Western Governments established military and scientific bases in the Arctic, they were prepared for the hazards of the intense cold – like living inside a refrigerator – and knew as a by-product that the freezing climate would at least preserve the food stores, which it did, slabs of meat staying frozen fresh for years. The unexpected trouble was, so did the human excreta; the 'honey buckets', as they were nicknamed, were emptied wherever possible and stayed where dumped – undissolved, a dark stain, year after year, they're still there. They can't be got rid of.

Have you ever considered how applicable this is also to a Yogi in the Himalayas, where the eternal snows would preserve all such excreta – for decades. How would a group survive in a true ashram, of the true Masters, the great Yogis, who dwell, always, above the snow line? There are no toilets, no rainy season.

Hence, the *preliminary* qualification of a neophyte is such control over his body, over his Chakras, over his 'Wheels', that cleansing as he seeks means in part the total, but total, cessation of the necessity for elimination.

Next time some fancy guru / teacher / holy man / pope / calif / son of god claims from you obedience, belief and homage – just check up on the toilet facilities in his private quarters! If he's got a toilet, he's not even passed the stage of Wheel 2, far far from Wheel 15, which itself, is yet of Manas (Mind) – two further stages of Love-Wisdom and the Supreme being even further on.

So, dear reader, you now have two verifiable checks – does the hair on the head 'stand out' with inner fire during the ceremony, and does he need a toilet!

This'll cut the numbers down a bit.

How is elimination made to cease?

Firstly, the higher Chakras when genuinely activated, take in the Life Forces of Prana, so that you don't have to feed solid food through the hole in the face (page 60)

secondly, the lower Chakras of Wheel One, have half their petals automatically activated, as explained on page 57, but the conscious, controlled, activation of the dormant half produces 'sublimation' at all levels – one being that the Pranic Life Forces intaken at the higher Chakras are exuded by a lower Chakra, in Law; neither the food intake nor the elimination outgo being dense physical. Hence elimination of urine / excreta ceases.

Mediator, is the technical term for such conscious occult power; the very opposite of the negative medium. A Mediator always is in conscious control, knows the

Law, the how/what, and has his petals of his Chakras accordingly under control.

So why be fooled? Hair on the head 'stands out', elimination ceased.

Mahatma Letter Number 49 (see end of book) has an illuminating passage at the close of several pages – long magnificent and deep Truths of answering questions and concluding with the throw-away line that the Master had 'remained for over nine days in his stirrups without dismounting'.

*Wheel 3*

and arithmetic has begun to give way to geometry.

*The Concentric Key* was known, used, and only thinly veiled by the great Mediator H. P. Blavatsky in her magnificent works like *The Secret Doctrine*. The jackals still howl round her heels but none who has actually studied that superb exposition of detailed/defined accurate Occult Laws in their application and use for us earthlings, no such researcher can know aught but admiration and gratitude for the enormous effort thus made to serve humanity. Jackals notwithstanding.

The Proof that H. P. Blavatsky used the Concentric Key, and impregnated the whole 1,474 pages of her work with it, is in the (*a*) abuse that the grey/black hurl at her, even now some ninety years after her death; and especially (*b*) in the haste with which they sought to destroy her book. This was done more subtly than the old-fashioned burning-at-a-stake:

*The Secret Doctrine* was published in December 1888; *before* even one copy had been seen the jackals howled.

The original edition sold out at once. The second (an exact copy) followed quickly, and sold rapidly, but at that period H. P. Blavatsky died – on 8 May, 1891.

People were clamouring for more copies. The plates for printing were there. Yet 'some' decided to withhold the book; they lost the profit; they paid the great cost of re-setting all the 1,474 pages of type; underwent the huge labour of re-writing and re-typing all that voluminous mass of technical and detailed facts; of entirely rewording the whole one thousand seven hundred and seventy-four pages! Why? What possible reason? Except to destroy the Concentric Key and the inner/deeper value of her work. *The Secret Doctrine* had been effectively removed from earthlings and would have stayed lost but for Robert Crosbie, who reprinted photographic exact copies of the original.

The same ruthless treatment was meted out to H. P. Blavatsky's other works and for the same reason; to all of them. Also to all, but all, the works of T. Subba Row, who also used/demonstrated the Concentric Key. The entire lot were rewritten – 'revised' was the euphemism – to eradicate all true indices of the sure steps to progress that the Concentric Key would high-light.

That's how important this Key is.

It has not been destroyed.

Earnest researchers are cordially invited to come and investigate. Incidentally, once fairly well mastered this Key can prove, yes prove, beyond argument whether a 'holy' book really is in total harmony with occult Law, or is merely 'man-made'. Imagine the effect on the fanatical adherents of any one of the dozen or so contenders for the title-holder of 'Up There' to have their 'sacred book' convincingly demonstrated to be less than perfect. You can understand the reluctance of 'some' to have the Concentric Key survive.

From Wheel 3 onwards arithmetic increasingly is expanded into this Concentric Key, to the Grand Geometrician of the Universe.

The 5 and the 6 rhythms are superimposed by a 3 x 7 to 'bed the rock' on which all, and yoga, stand.

The well-known Kundalini Serpent fire starts to uncoil – and woe to the occultist who focuses only from Wheel 3.

Meditation vivifies. Midnight starts. The Quabalistic Red starts.

Wisdom 10 – 12 starts.

*Wheel 4* sees Purple – occultly. It reaches the 'full moon of June' – the sixth month.

The 6⇌9 transformation ARE

The first Nirvana IS, as dawns the 'full moon of July', the seventh 'month'.

5 ; 3 x 6.

*Wheels 5 to 15* continue the story of true yoga, of its permeation in One-ness, finally reaching the Most High; Truth.

Obvious, as said, a full exposition in writing would neither be practical nor prudent.

But yoga is; the way for you is; the time for you is.

Let's start now.

*Fivefold clues*

The rhythm of 5 has been mentioned. In part it naturally refers to the plane of Manas, Mind. 5+5+5 in its 3 stages.

The Gautama Buddha enjoined the Five precepts; which were to abstain from:

1. destruction of life (for example, by hostile thoughts)
2. theft (for example, not giving full effort to your task)
3. falsehood (lacking moral courage / true vision)
4. sexual impurity (including desire / thought)
5. intoxicants which cloud the mind (prejudices)

Each has many levels, clearly

each affects many petals, of many Chakras.

Beauty unfolds; Life IS. Yoga IS

The Concentric Key has not been lost.

Try using it, coupled with the above, to plot your own way through the maze, to reach the dizzy Truth of *Right* motive (the master key) and to know enough, deeply enough, in the full fivefold pattern of the above Precepts, to know, actually know, that what you thought was the right motive, was in occult fact – right!

# PART THREE
# *MEDITATION*

## 6. Essential

Like Yoga, like Occult, Meditation also interpenetrates, and permeates One-ness; to separate any part from the whole is artificial, and does not co-work with the invisible, hidden noumenon – the interior cause – of the exterior effect.

The superficial forms of body yoga (Hatha) that gives physical exercise and relaxation are widespread and beneficial at that level; so too with popular meditation which merely quietens the body/emotions/lower mind and thus encourages a gentle sense of (outer) peace; this, too, is well known, and is, too, beneficial at that level.

True meditation is all powerful, it is yoga in action, it, too, is the art mode of inner speech referred to on page 67. By its operation gives power to free-range a solar system, and far more. Western incredulity notwithstanding. The 'way' of such true Meditation, the 'aim' of such true yoga, the 'motive' of such true Occultism is 'the same and the other' to use a technical term. All three being alone-begotten, Self born (not self born), according to the innermost occult sound (technical term) of the aspirant.

Since the (being re-discovered and no longer lost) Concentric Key is not so geometrically evident in Meditation, and since the Yoga section was mainly for the studious researcher or for the deeply thoughtful, let us consider meditation in its more-outer aspects in the hope

77

that you, dear reader, will be encouraged to apply them to your living-life;

because a change for the better will surely follow, if you do.

The keynote, as always, is unselfishness of motive: the purer the motivating impulse, the finer the flow; the more separated the thought, the greater the kick-back – on you. In full.


Section 1. *Still-essential*

Negative meditation is not, positively not, recommended.

It is stupid, plain stupid, to rely on exterior guidance/ inspiration/ impulse. You would not hand over your physical body to an unknown driver-in-a-car who could wreck it;

to hand over your physical+etheric+desire-mind+ Life forces bodies to an unknown infinitely is more hazardous;

to rely on some outside guru/god is the way of the lazy cheat – you can't be bothered to make your own path; feel inadequate (lazy) to forge it gradually life after life; are greedy to have instant results now from some Sat-Guru/Holy He-god;

and anyway, have 'better' and more 'practical' things to do, and can't/won't start to begin to commence to walk – with perseverance, with moderation, with discrimination – the long long road. Alone.

Frankly, you had better leave meditation alone. Stick to 'prayer' in some accepted/organized/exoteric comfort. Just relax and deep breathe. And vegetate!

Let's hope that made you cross; let's hope you use the surge of energy of 'cross' not at others but inwards to spurt you on to Meditation.


Section 2. *The start*

So, with you in charge; you alone in control; always and invariably;

with positive alertness, with no single hint of passive

acceptance;

let us commence meditation with our seven bodies –
the 'lower four' in incarnation (physical, etheric, desire-
mind, Life forces); plus the timeless triad of the higher-
mind, the Love-Wisdom, the Supreme.

Let's first put the lower four bodies in a chair, and seat
them comfortably.

## Stage 1

1. feet flat on the floor, firm; earthed.
2. buttocks well back into the seat of the chair;
anchored.
3. spine erect. Not taut, but definitely erect. Any
tendency to imbalance should be corrected; now; so that
it does not lean forward/back to the left/right. Erect.
4. head erect. No strain, but as if gently and firmly
drawn upwards; straight upwards, neither right nor left,
forward not back. Truly erect.

Chin in. Please don't jut it forward as the head may tilt
back.

Firm, alert: without strain.

Intensely alive, relaxed. Aware.

Meditation, like Yoga, like Occultism has to be honest;
be true. In the early stages your body may not obey you,
and may lean off balance without your knowing; it may
almost as easily fool the practised meditator who might
even kid himself that he is long past this stage of physical
balance.

So, please do check. In a mirror, or have someone you
can trust gently ease the head/spine/chin/shoulders into
erect, firm, easy balance.

Perhaps you would like to practise that for five to ten
minutes a day; every day; regularly.

## Stage 2

What did you do with your hands during stage 1?
Earthlings as they go through Life, 'walk' they call it,
waddle and flap as their differentiated legs jerk to the left
of the point of balance, or to the right (seldom at balance
itself!) and so too with their loose/flappy arms.

So what did you do with yours? and your shoulders?

At ease, relaxed, hands flat on the thighs or quietly folded (not clapsed/gripped/jammed in interlock) on the lap; shoulders relaxed, even.

If so you had probably got your etheric body nicely fluffed and neatly arranged round the chair; it too, at ease, erect, firm, alert, alive. Not passive, drooped, or fidgety.

Why not try now, again, for another five to ten minutes, each and every never-missed, day. Perhaps too at a regular time.

The lower four bodies are repetitive creatures, liking to do the same thing over and over again, typical of the half-grown child-like are they. Incidentally, are you in a rut? When did you buy different newspapers? Say something original? Change your routine/patter/habit? Are you one of those Kama-Manas (see page 38) prisoners that use give-away expressions like 'I always this . . . I never that'?

'Cos otherwise you're not the boss – your desire-mind body (Kama-Manas) has got you twiddled round its little finger, and is roaring its head off in amusement as you think you're meditating. You're simply the puppet, dangling as always to its whim.

Meditation, like Yoga, like Occult, has to be honest, be true.

This business of alertness, of (inner) balance is deeper than might at first be thought.

The more the interior – and exterior – gathering together, the more genuine the alive/alert state, relaxed 'and full', the more likely is meditation to begin;

as permeation through and through 'itself' begins to radiate – in scope, in time, in space. Truth, real truth, ever is gently in harmony, alert-ease, balance.

Outer things quieten. Inner forces stir.

A sense of One-ness with the room, the surrounding, begins genuinely to flow – the forced pretence is worse than useless, is down right retrograde – as does a linking awareness with people, with things, with no things. Discords give way as they are seen to be actually what they are – having at least a triple relationship of you, of the

external-stimuli, and of the discord itself; and of the reason
for the discord; and that reason will be much deeper than
the obvious (rather white-washed) one that first presented
itself for occult view.

Stillness stirs.

Some meditators now like to inject a 'seed-thought' of
virtue / attribute / ethics. Please please please don't start
wallowing in syrup / love of some exoteric fancy / system /
guru-god. Alert. You ALONE creating, you ALONE in
charge. Always.

The seed-thought obviously will be inclusive – not you
lot come and join my lot; that filthy word 'my' stinks
of selfishness, of separateness. With it meditation
positively is not.

The all permeating seed thought, utterly utterly
impersonal, as applicable to earthlings as to Space Peoples
in other planets, to the formless / wholeness of Life, all
Life – such seed thoughts focus away from the thing-
meditating-on-the-chair to Timeless Truth.

Perhaps you would like to try this, regularly, perhaps
even in the same place as well as the same time – for
five or ten lives. Yes, lives.

Do you remember page 71, the stage of Wheel 2 when
'the hair is cut'? It was at that (vast) stage that the true
Hierophant's hair 'stood out' as the inner forces activated
it – the Christian halo of inner electric forces radiating –
so, what happened to your hair? Is it still flat and
plastered down? A sobering thought.

No gurus / gods in garlands, expensive cars, fancy
Cathedrals / Mosques / Temples, or even in pent-house suites
complete with Public Relation Officers can fool you – what
did your hair do when you meditated? Stand-out it will;
when in truth Wheel 2 operates – when you alone, by
yourself, DO.

Next time you have some fancy-titled, fancy-dressed
show-off demanding obedience, adulation and offerings –
look at the hair. In the fulness of the ceremony / ritual /
meditation / chant / prayer – did it stand-out? No wonder
so many of them cover it; the more gorgeous, the more
traditional, the more distracting the head-gear; the better –

for them. You may as well also check on the toilet facilities, of the Holy Man (page 73) while you're at it!

Meanwhile, let's persevere; in moderation; in balance.

*Stage 3*

is of great opportunity, great responsibility, great danger. A deliberate activation of the Prana, Life Forces, to play through the Kama-Manas (desire-mind) + the etheric + the physical.

Results come forth. With a vengence. As very lightly outlined for Wheel 3 of Yoga.

But it is here that you, the alone-begotten, the one free creative agent in Nature, you, unaided, by your own unique occult note, you have to 'bed the rock on which all will stand'; Midnight starts, and should lead to Dawn, Enlightenment; as the 'Red' (blood / essence / dhatu / flame) leads to 'Purple', the Patrician mark of the Noble Roman, the Senator, the Lawgiver, the Ruler – you.

Activating your Kama (Desire / emotion) as your purify / sublimate so that it changes from the personalized e-motion to the neuter wholeness, all-embracing motion, pure throb of the Universe; seat of the Lipika Webs (technical term) in their triple flow of the Spiral (Truth), of the Concentric (Concentric Key; grand geometrician) and of the Linear (arithmetic, the great architect, the razor-edged path). A throb here touched / sensed / roused.

Popularized as Kundalini fire. Of itself really dangerous, and unusable.

The second prong of Kama-Manas is of course, Mind, Full Mind 'of the 15 Wheels', essentially, vitally essential to balance the first prong, the Universal throb – motion.

It is little use prattling about 'stilling the mind'; 'going beyond the mind'.

Without Manas no-thing IS, not even you, let alone the galaxies. The famous generic keynote of 'Patanjali', that has spanned the true Yoga for at least 5,000 millennia (sorry!) speaks of 'modifications of the thinking principle' and of 'pure as rock-crystal'.

So in stage 3 of meditation, when deciding which Pranic Life Forces are to be spurted-into-result, at which level, in which way, we need first to understand the Thinking Principle, Manas; and its modifications. Everything in the entire ranges of Universes is alive (scientists can faint now), and in this manvantara (technical term) of 4,320,000,000 years are sevenfold; including Manas.

As this living, Thinking Principle ebbs and flows over its sevenfold vastnesses, its lower / denser / personalized as I am I / desire part becomes repetitive – as Kama-Manas (desire-mind), and gets bogged down in 'sandbanks of thought' (Samskaras is the technical term). The range is far wider than the sub-conscious to super-conscious stuff of the outer / visible man / nation, and to be understood needs the Mind that can span the 770 lives of page 33; a Mind that ranges over the seven bodies, including at least the Sixth, if not the Seventh.

To travel this long unravel-of-the thread we need to start by recognizing what is not of the Real, not of Permanent; the not-this, not-that process of elimination to strip the pious dross of our forebears (that is, of ourselves in former lives). Psychology helps only / solely at the dense / low levels. Next the occult schools that seek to eliminate the 'Various I's' that clutter me, in this life.

Truth; moderation; discrimination; perseverance finally will lead to an understanding of the sandbanks of thought that have modified the free flow of the Thinking Principle that have caused distortions, prejudices, weaknesses, fears, and pain, and from this realization of these sandbanks eventually / instantly, comes their elimination.

Concentration, right concentration, added to the four qualities of the sentence above, lead to the activation of Wheel 5, to a 'freedom' from (lower) mind, and pave the ways (sevenfold) to contemplation, to comprehension; Dharana, Dhyana, Samadhi, each sevenfold, being the well-known technical terms.

But this state of consciousness is not reached from the lower, repetitive mind; nor from the (ahamkara) bridge of I am I; but inwards towards, at least to approach the pure rock crystal;
    all-round,
    whole, undistorted, pure

with you *inside* the sphere, right right in the inmost centre 'which is no-where, everywhere'.

Do it right and Omnipotence, Omniscience, Omnipresence is yours, as your hair stands out, as elimination ceases, as you free range the galaxies – past, present, future – with a Mind-to-embrace-the-Universe (technical term). Be Space Peoples in short. Do it wrong, and you pay the price.

In full.

And then start again. Better this time. Because there's always hope, and time and opportunity; because we ourselves, by ourselves, through ourselves make it.

Sevenfold Samadhi IS/ARE

It's a longish way – Let's start now.


SECTION 3. *Some elementary ground-rules*

*Relaxation*

starts from the periphery towards the centre, from the extremites reaching to the head; the better to get 'the currents' energized 'the right way' – towards the within, the noumenon, the hidden cause; the outer effects will take care of themselves if the inner state is 'right'.

Thus, relax the toes, each one, separately, in the 'right' order (which you have to decide, in discrimination),

then the ankles,

the calf, the leg, the thighs

simultaneously, because 'Full Manas' has 15 wheels and can work at several planes/states/time at once (even we earthlings can drive a car and talk at the same moment), you also relax:

*The Sevenfold Hand*

the fingers, in the 'right' order, one at a time. At least we all know this one – just contemplate your own hand:

the little finger, away off at the 'bottom' – representing the physical body. The least 'important', the furthest away from the centre;

next the finger you girls put your engagement or

84

wedding rings on. *Why* on this one? It's the beginning of
the inner bodies, the 'soul contact', so that men 'will still
love you when you're old'; it represents the etheric body.
It's bigger than the (physical) little-finger, far wider
ranging, and the physical has been built 'in its image',
as you brought through your etheric-mould from a
previous life – or fresh out of Celestial Sugar Daddy's
factory if you prefer that sort of story – no doubt because
you happen to have been born into it, have been
indoctrinated (Kama-Manas *likes* the repetitive, the
familiar) and have never bothered to get all 15 Wheels
activated in Full Mind, in Freedom, including freedom of
(original) thought – that is, because you've probably
never really bothered to think deeply about it. That old
'devil' of the anthropomorphics (the He-gods: Jewish,
Christian and Moslem – in chronological order) must be
the biggest scrap dealer of the local galaxies with the
souls that end up dumped; his turn-over must put our
multi-national Big Business to shame. Let's hope he doesn't
pollute the galaxies by scattering 'disposables' like we do.
Perhaps Sugar Daddy could re-cycle the waste products.

Next comes the biggest finger of them all, the one that
most motivates us earthlings at this time, i.e. since the
Fall into matter of Lemuria, when we first got a physical
body as spirit conjoined with matter, to give duality,
i.e. for the past few 18,000,000 years, ever since we had
a desire-mind (Kama-Manas) body. Our emotions, bless
them; powerful, capable of subliminating to Heights – but
ruled by mind? controlled by mind? In check / ontrack /
at the centre? Hence our difficulties with meditation and
with relaxation, as the inherent life force in our fingers /
toes / eye-brows fidgets and distracts as it resists efforts to
channel it into controlled / regulated ways.

Then the 'fourth state' as represented by the top finger,
the index finger; by the boss finger, we hope, that rules
the others in Law and Harmony, as is 'mostly' (higher)
mind rather than 'mere' desire-mind, and is the clue /
index for the activation of the Life Forces of Prana
surging the 15 Wheels: Serene mind, still mind, living
and vibrant and alert and controlling – the very very

opposite of passive/negative, of blind (stupid?) 'acceptance of what comes'.

A positive, a vital, a knowing link to:

the triple thumb (look at it again, please note its three divisions, two big, one narrow).

Let us please now ponder over an extraordinary fact that has happened. When focused on the fingers our consciousness was in line with the 'direction they pointed', i.e. left to right; in permeation with the room, the surrounds, with the planet; with things, with people, with no-things.

Now, suddenly/instantly/in a flash of enlightenment we have 'jumped the gap' from 'left to right', and now point at right-angles (a fourth part of a circle) to point 'up-down' – when the thumb is 'raised'. Something none, but none, of the other fingers can do, that *cannot* be reached in the four states of consciousness represented by them.

We are now 'in full Manas', having changed 'I am I' to 'am' (by absorbing-in both the separative/selfish 'I' of the joint higher-and-the-lower sides of am).

Am, can now operate, that is, *a* (the first vowel, the initial impulse of energy, the Word/the Vach/the Celestial Song) and *m* the middle consonant of the alphabet, the market place/the physical focus-out-in-(controlled)-action.

Am-ness IS

A U M, O M, IS

Meditation is.

Let's leave the two other (and even 'broader' divisions of the thumb), the Sixth and Seventh bodies/states to 'another day another time'.

Relaxation then is interior. It is not, repeat not, a deadening, a suffocation, a preventing, a thou-shalt-not.

It is first a realization of the sandbanks of repetitive thought/fidgets that inhibit, that modify (distort) the gentle permeation of the all-embrancing Thinking Principle.

It is a seeing of things as they are. True seeing. An acknowledgement. Not, repeat not, a pretending that things are other than they are, a wish to change them, to remove them. Such will follow in ordered Law, as we realize, deeply and in truth, the modification of the Thinking Principle.

First we relax; we see; we see through and through and through – things as actually ex-isting (us-them-no-thing) – and in that alive-alert-conscious-knowing sense alone we 'accept'.

But But But, this is not passive. It is we/you alone who sees, who is in control, who changes.

It is you alone who can sound your inmost occult sound – your own 'vowel A'.

*Breathing*

Meanwhile what has happened to your breath? – the physical vowel A.

Of 'its own accord' it should have slowed down by now, have quietened

have deepened

as inner richer states of awareness ARE.

The pauses between the in-breath, and the out-breath may well have become imperceptibly but significantly more marked; of increasing duration.

as All-breath replaces gradually the dual in-or-separated-out breaths.

Gradually, over 5 or 10 lives

In truth.

If all you've done is to 'count your breath', to 'hold your breath' you'll end up purple in the face –

nothing like the 'see Purple Occultly of Wheel 4' (page 75)

It'll be time to start again.

It'll be time to remember Wheel 2 (page 71 to 73) towards the fruition of which the automatic half of the Chakras 'without action' was complemented by the Mediator (conscious control) activation of the dormant half so that they became 'with action', so that the breath ceased to be in or out, separated, but the unified/linked/yogic All Breath. The analogy there given of sublimating solid food to Pranic Life Forces having the result of continuous cleaning at inner Chakra level thus obviating elimination, holds good for breath, your personal vowel A.

It has many other results too, all tending to Occult Purple, beckoning you on to truer Meditation.

Let's start now.

*Concentration – identification – detachment*
The serious researcher will have long since realized the importance of concentration, especially if 'right', and should reach heights of powers able to construct on a sublime scale.

More modest beginnings are often urged by focusing the mind; a lower attribute, say on a box, a painting, a flower – some relatively easily recognized and remembered object;

to focus the (lower) mind so that it does not wander off, does not leave / forget / deviate from the object, even when you have ceased to look with your physical eyes, which you have closed and are visualizing the object on your mental screen. Alternating: from view, pause, visualize; and later to 'remember'; you'll be shattered at how much you didn't, at first, but rapidly should improve.

Hard work, of course; necessary, of course. Taking years of perseverance. If done in Truth, then Life improves, even with this one simple exercise; but perseverance and discrimination are big words!

Exercise 2 is then to focus the mind so that no stray thoughts filter through, and the focus stays alive / exact.

Again, the totality of Life will improve, if done in Truth, to an even more impressive degree; over the years of application. All sorts of cheap gimmicks are offered: if a thought strays in – then mentally go and fetch it back; or mentally trace where it came from, reaching back from the moment of entry in your mind. Why are these two (well-known) gimmicks cheap? They have both merely encouraged you to break focus, and to 'go off somewhere'.

Perseverance and discrimination are big words!

Exercise 3 invites a complete identification, utter blending into one, with the object, say a flower, so that 'you' cease as a separate entity and fully are permeated into the flower. You are that flower.

As an exercise, it is valid, is important, and yet again will improve the wholeness of Life. It too will take years.

All three exercises can be done each day/hour/minute/year.

As a skilled pianist enjoys and revels in his play, you may do likewise with the enormous openings these new strengths inevitably will bring. And now comes the danger.

Motive. Right motive. Selfless – not selfish, nor even separative. Otherwise woe follows in full proportion.

But so too does Truth, in equally full proportion, if your motive is pure, and you are 'non-attached' – you do what is right, because it is right; and you have enough discrimination to know it is right. That's even harder.

And it leads even further!

*The 'easy' way*
Abundantly clear from all the above is the need for hard work – pure motive.

Many a 'Guru', many a school/system offers easy ways/instant success. Follow that Guru, chant that mantra – Ram, the Indian folk-god, for instance – and it's 'all yours; no need to change your ways, no need to work'.

Well somebody's fooling! 'Patanjali Yoga' is several million years old, with some of the loftiest Beings of the 'Golden Thread' who have served humanity; if there had been an easy way to Truth, you'd think they'd have known. Even the Buddha had to sweat it out.

'Get rich quick' does not only apply to gold; harm done on the inner planes may take more than one life to repair.

Discrimination is always a big word.

# PART FOUR
# *FLYING SAUCERS*

## Essential

It is now well over a quarter of a century since the modern story began in 1947; several hundred books have been written; more than 3,000 earth people are known to have had contact with the occupants of landed Saucers, many many more are estimated to have kept quiet and to be continuing their meetings – 'only the failures and martyrs are known';

Eight governments have admitted the reality of Saucers.

Photos, films, colour films, radar fixes (ground and airborne, and both simultaneously), landing marks, crushed vegetation, altered soil composition at the site, residue – all exist in superabundance;

demonstrations over towns, even repeated same time / same place / same height for twenty-one days; groups of Saucers, formations, of the sixteen known and catalogued different types;

famous people who have publicly admitted to seeing Saucers; ambassadors, senators, tycoons, police, 26 astronauts since 1962, astronomers, astro-physicists, pilots, State Governors, and huge cross-sections of the population; let us restate – 26 astronauts who have seen / photographed / filmed on Apollo II, on Skylab II, on Skylab III during 1962–1974;

the National Opinion Polls regularly have sampled (and who *paid* for these expensive tests, regularly taken)

91

and consistently have shown since 1956 that more and more people believed in Saucers. By 1973 the staggering proportion of two out of three accepted their existence.

Did you know?

Or had you been one of the ever-diminishing laggards (?!!) – two out of three accept Saucers – who had:

1. decried them as non-proven
2. dismissed them as unimportant
3. shrugged them off with some glib 'explanation' such as saviour-myth, hallucination, mistaken for natural phenomena, psychic vagaries.

If so, would you please like to re-consider. Please read on.

Flying Saucers are very serious business indeed. They will/do affect every major aspect of our lives, right down to the very marrow of the bones of our thoughts/ feelings/outlook.

They are here to help us help ourselves. Not to do the dirty work for us lazy lot – 'why don't THEY land in Hyde Park' the unthinking were wont to say – but to show us how to reach up/through:

into the New Age

by our own efforts.

No wonder 'some' decry them as 'hostile'. But two out of three don't!

It's a fascinating story. Let's start now.


*Fundamental first step*

First things first. The galaxy is bigger than this village, planet earth – so too may be its concepts and knowledge;

the galaxy is older than this mud of ours – so too may be its growth, and its range of perception. Why should it be limited merely to our five tiny senses?

the galaxy (just the local one) has more habitable planets than we have houses. Why should all its multi-faceted Life Forms be shrunk into a lop-sided little body like earthlings (pages 14 to 15)?

It is we who have to grow to the stature of the galaxy;

not scream that THEY squeeze their multi-millions of gallons into our pint pot.

It's time for us to expand our vision. Let's start now.

# 7. Historical Survey, 1947-74

*Section I*

These twenty-seven years saw a great change, in five
distinct developments, recognizable in spite of overlaps.
Summarized only now, and then considered in detail over
the next thirty pages.

1. 1947–54: open discussion of the subject, with evidence
galore featuring in the news media.

2. 1954: silence. Abruptly the stories vanished from
the press of England, America, Europe; and even, more
difficult to understand, also vanished simultaneously from
the press of Russia, China, Africa and Asia. Two hours'
work in a reference library will prove this unbelievable
fact.

Were the major governments contacted by the Saucers,
as the persistent stories insist? At Muroc, the Edwards
Air Force Base? Details below.

3. Ridicule (officially inspired?) of any who dared to
relate their sighting, their photo/film/landing marks/
contact.

4. When the surging mass of continuing evidence by
credible witnesses/radar/films could no longer be ridiculed
to silence, then came the spate of 'conventional
explanations', of all (but an irritating residue) being
explainable as natural phenomena.

5. When the drivel about space debris, falling meteorites,

93

mock suns, ball lightning, temperature inversions, cloud-reflections/spots before the eyes/saviour myth hallucinations/marsh gas/high flying geese/refuelling planes, etc., etc., all wore thin in the face of hard factual reality then came, in the late 1960s to the early 1970s, an increasing admission that Saucers were real – eight governments openly admitting this – but an hysterical shriek of Saucers being hostile, of abducting, of kidnapping. Extraordinary was this frantic smear – which Truth just does not substantiate. After all, have you been conquered yet? They've been around since 1947, or since the Pharaohs of Ancient Egypt who recorded them on their official Papyri, as do the Christians in their Bible, the Hindus in their Vedah – some 5,000 B.C. There seems very little conquest to show after all those years!

Now, let's look in great detail, and especially at the Government contact in spring 1954 at Muroc, Edwards Air Force Base.


SECTION 2. *1947–54* Open discussion. *Lessons to learn*

The expression 'Flying Saucers' was embedded into the consciousness of humanity by the Kenneth Arnold sighting of 1947, and has defied all attempts to dislodge it – everyone right round the planet is aware of the expression and that surely is unique. After all the 'Holy Bible' may be no more recognized in a Hindu bazaar than their 'Sacred Baghavad Gita' is in the High Street supermarket, but everyone, everywhere, knows 'flying saucers'. Staggering, when you come to think about it.

Its appeal is simple, is all-inclusive – both hallmarks of Deep Truth – and the poorest peasant, illiterate and starving, still knows what a saucer is, and what flying is, be he in jungle, forest, swamp, or in darkest Piccadilly. No one is left out – as they are by the fancy stuff of 'Unidentified Flying Object' of those snooty ones who sought an expression that was more dignified, more impressive, more authoritative.

Also more separative – and therein lies the rub; lesson number one is that Saucers include all us earthlings in our total, not just picking and choosing bits of our village, planet earth. One-ness IS.

June 24, 3 p.m., 1947, at Mount Rainier, Washington State, was the scene of the Kenneth Arnold sighting in bright sunshine, of the nine objects – 'skimming like Flying Saucers' manoeuvring at 'impossible' speeds in and out of the mountain peaks, in loose formations that inevitably would led to collisions even if earth craft could have reached such speeds; all the while dazzling within-out colour changes from purest white ('silver', within-out, white) through greens, blues, reds – marvellous to behold. The clear, concise, detailed report of a trained pilot, airborne himself, created an undying impression; which has stuck.

Yet, a deeper realization has increased over the years that humanity has missed the real significance of that event, in looking merely at the outer facts of speed, height, changes of course, colour, shape, mountains, and so on.

Truth may well lie deeper for those who have eyes to see:

Kenneth Arnold was piloting his own plane; thus he was successful enough in business to buy one, also his air training and skill were impeccable, and all that 'inspires confidence', 'wins approval' – and is typical of the earthling reactions for those still on the downward into matter arc (page 32), the selfish arc. At the time of the sighting Kenneth was on a mercy mission; helping to look for a missing plane; helping his fellow man; with no thought of reward – action of the return arc of evolution back to One-ness. That was *why* he was allowed to have the sighting; because nothing is of chance in this type of contact

Please, please reconsider page 42/43, where Full Mind, Full Manas is discussed, in which 'all the minds that influenced the mind of the author when he wrote the book are known instantly'. This is typical of the Mind of the advanced Space peoples, as we shall see later on page 120, such instantaneous and such full Knowledge, with freedom of time travel and hence of pre-vision, precludes the 'chance encounter' for events of this magnitude. Please also let's consider all the other factors so far overlooked, albeit available from the data given, that is, from the Saucer demonstration, for those who have eyes to see; nothing was 'by chance':

1. The date was June 24, 1947.

June is the Sixth month of the year, symbolic of the Sixth Root Race of Man, of the future; of the Sixth Body of Man (page 40) of Love-Wisdom;

of the sixth sense of man, taking him beyond the mere five.

June is mid-summer, when the (Higher) Solar Forces are at their peak and the (lower) Lunar energies are at their ebb.

24 is a very powerful, occult, combination of numbers, for example,

Double-Twelve, of the shadow / substance, darkness / light, – 12 inches, 12 hours, 12 apostles – 12 signs of the Zodiac, 12 inner petals of the Crown Chakram (page 57);

or the 3 (trinity) x 8 of Buddha's Noble Eightfold Path (symbology is not just meant for Christians!) of the Eight points of the Compass (page 70); of 9 (3+3+3. that is, the 30+1+1+1 to give the 33° or the 'age of Jesus, who was "33" ', the sign of an Initiate)+15 (The 15 Wheels of Full Manas, as on page 65), etc.

1947 added up comes to 21, i.e. to 3 (trinity) x 7 planes of consciousness; or seven bodies of Man; 7 Chakras; etc.

2. The local time was 3 p.m.

Another trinity, in the glory of the solar forces, as the physical sun shone bright and clear.

3. Where was the sighting? At Mount Rainer. A mountain of spirit as distinct from the vale of matter has been symbolic as such since the dawn of time.

4. What's special about Mount Rainer?

It has three peaks – trinity, be they the Christian, be they Shiva, Vishnu, Brahma of 5000 B.C. of the Hindus, be they Osiris, Horus and Troth of the Pharaohs of more. much more, than 12000 B.C.

5. What were the Saucers doing?

Going in and out of the three-trinity-peaks of the mountain – spirit; rubbing Humanity's nose in the symbolism.

6. How many Saucers were there?

Nine. The number of self-initiation, of he who has yet to raise himself to the 10 of perfection, of a Plato, of a Pythagoras. Nine seems more appropriate an aim for humanity, not yet wholly past the turning point (page 25) from involution down into matter back upwards on the return arc to One-ness.

7. What was happening at 3 p.m. on that day?

An extraordinary cluster of planets at the high noon of 'MC', with only one below the rising arc, all the rest in the top of the chart magnificently arranged, with Jupiter (Higher Mind, Full Manas) and Venus (Love-Wisdom) prominent in their interplay.

Now was all that an accident? Or was there much, below the obvious, for those who have eyes to see.

The lessons for Humanity are there to learn – at ever deeper levels

by our own efforts

at every sphere of consciousness.

What about the colours? what about their meaning, depicting as they do the inner sounds, the inner Word, the inner powers. Do you really think they were just pretty lights, mere toys, or mere index of speed accelerating to – beyond the speed of light / visibility. As Saucers often do. Nuts-and-bolts chaps who say 'nothing can exist beyond the speed of light' please re-examine,

in seven planes,

in seven bodies.

Let's start now.


Section 3. *1947–54 Landing Contacts*

Over 3,000 known contacts, repeat known, with landed Saucers and their occupants; in every continent, every culture, every nation (England too!); please see some of the several hundred books for details, as suggested at the end of this one.

What was the common characteristic of the earthling that made the contact? Do *you* know? Or had you just dismissed the whole lot as nonsense – without even learning the names of say a typical 50 cases, let alone having read their stories, or having interviewed them. Such is rejection in ignorance and prejudice; characteristics of the downward-into-matter arc, of these who cling to the known, who hug their comfort/security/Medals/Fame and is – stupid! Those who have such a retrograde attitude, are those who themselves form the bulk of the laggards who still reject Saucers – two out of three people accept them – and have a common characteristic too! Very easily recognized are these retrogrades – they all tend to over use the words 'I' 'me' 'myself' 'personally': separative words, selfish; that may well bring their user Power/Fame/Authority, but seldom lead to Saucer contacts, or to One-ness/Truth. Such self-centred laggards are clearly of the involution-into-matter down-ward arc. It's time to 'turn', past the turning point. Let's start now.

So, what was the common factor of those earthlings who did make Saucer contacts? It was not the obvious outer-only form-only stuff like – open-air types, science fiction addicts, simple/gullible/unimportant; included were the young, the old; the Western, the Eastern; the man, boy, woman, child; peasant and sophisticate – all.

All, too, seemed to ask the same question of the Space People – why contact me, I'm nobody; why not go to the President/Prime Minister/Archbishop/Scientist, etc.? Space Peoples always replied 'we don't choose you, you choose us' or, you have reached a state of consciousness where you can stand the sudden heightening of the inner bodies, and of Kundalini Fire (technical term, see page 82) thus caused. If you're discounting this, then please face one question:

Why was Jesus not born Caesar at Rome? Presumably, as the 'son of god' he could have; presumably he knew how much more authoritative that would have been – so why not do it? Krishna was only a Shepherd; Buddha was not on the Peacock Throne at Delhi, Why? Zarathustra, Osiris, Narayana – all gods, say their stories

98

– none were born 'caesar in Rome'. Were they all daft – or have we missed the true point?

Please think. Please consider carefully what might happen to you if Jesus suddenly materialized in your room, or a Space Man dropped in for tea. What would be the result on your seven bodies, especially the etheric, the emotions – the every-day mind? Very very few of us could take the shock of an abrupt raising of forced-by-an-outside-stimulus surge of consciousness, of an (unprepared) uncoiling of the Kundalini fire. As it is, 'only failures and martyrs of the contactees are known,' those that did not sustain the shock – in spite of their common characteristic which, by now you may have discovered.

Basically, all contactees have the inner gentleness, the inner strength, the inner unfoldment of those who have struggled past the turning point to the return arc in a sufficient degree to:

(a) make a contact 'possible'

(b) to have a reasonable chance of surviving the shock, and of going on to deeper levels.

Most did survive. Only the failures and martyrs are known; any weakness, in the lower bodies, and fuse blows as the Interior Fires light, as the Wheels (page 71) activate: the show-off, the liar, the coward, the greedy, etc. – all these fuses-blown are visible in the 'failures'. The greater the credit to those who succeeded.

If Jesus had been born Caesar, and had become authoritative, and had enforced his sayings with the power of the armed Legions – would any of that really have helped 'you' to turn from involution down-into-matter back to the return arc of One-ness, from hate to Harmony?

Would that have made 'you' change from selfish to One-ness, from take-to-give, from fear to Harmony?

Gentle, true, inner strength earthlings who do *not* over use 'I' 'me' 'myself' 'personally' – how often do such selfless ones become Prime Minister / President / Archbishop / Scientist?

How many Cathedrals did Jesus have? How many

gorgeous clothes, golden ornaments, fancy titles?

To repeat, the Saucer Peoples say 'we don't choose you, you choose us.'


SECTION 4. *1947–54 Lessons from Contacts*

The reader unfamiliar with stories of meetings with Space Beings, may care to brush up with some of the books listed at the end, but let us now take two stories, both well known, and see if there is more than meets the (superficial) eyes; if there are lessons for humanity to learn.

Everyone seems to have heard of the George Adamski contact in the Arizona desert on 20 November, 1952, arranged by telepathy subsequent to years of 'sky watch for Saucers' and to consequent self-preparation. The central event of the contact was that the Venusian, wearing specially engraved shoes, made footprints in the sand, sufficiently deep for a plaster cast to be taken of the embedded-clearly-in-the-sand prints. Researchers afterwards took an earthling to the identical spot, put football boots with heavy indentations on their soles on his feet, and told him to press down into the sand so as to make imprints clear-cut enough for a plaster cast to be taken. The earthling utterly failed to be able to bed down hard enough, although he was of the same height and apparent weight as the Venusian. The superficial investigators felt this proved Adamski to be a fraud; as usual, the Venusians themselves just waited patiently for earthlings to look deeper;

Adamski had done his self preparation for contact by years of 'sky watch' and of study. On 22 August, 1953, nine months later the nine of self-initiation (pages 57 and 59) Salvador Villanueva Medina proved his self-preparation, as had Kenneth Arnold, by charitable acts and thoughts to fellow beings in trouble, and had his contact:

his taxi broke down 300 miles north of Mexico City at Valles, in a deserted spot of course – Venusians don't allow 'well attested with (unprepared) witnesses', to the

100

fury of the sceptics – and he was forced to spend the rainy night in his cab. Three strangers approached in the darkness – three – and Medina, of his own kindness, offered them shelter inside his taxi from the rain. Some people might have bolted the (stable, no room at the inn) doors to unknown men in dark places, but Medina proved on this occasion that he had passed the turning point and had the inner strength/gentleness/trust of the return arc to merit his chance of a contact;

the three turned out to be Venusians and they offered to take Medina to their landed Saucer, which could be seen at dawn to be stationary 300 yards away;

across swampy ground. The Venusians walked across, without sinking up to their ankles as did Medina, following behind. They walked, as do all Initiates, as did Jesus, 'on the waters'. (The tame psychologists will claim that this proved they were hallucinations; as did the above sceptics claim that Adamski's Space-prints prove him to be a fake!!)

Let us look deeper.

In Adamski's case the Venusians made their bodies heavier than we can, in Medina's they did the reverse. They demonstrated, as have done yogis, Initiates, and the 'Golden-Thread of Evolutionary return arc Beings', control of the physical body – from the inner six bodies: etheric, desire-mind (Kama-Manas), Life forces (Prana); full Manas, Love-Wisdom, Supreme. Please please do reconsider the Occult facts in Part I of this book.

It is a lesson we all have to master, in one life or another. 'Gods' make/materialize/project bodies at will, say the stories. So can Venusians. So can 'you'. Even Hatha Yoga as done on the stage in the West can 'will a body to be so heavy' that four strong men fail to lift a girl. Fire walking, levitating, crossing waters – all are quite quite possible – using the interior focus on inner bodies – for 'you'.

Please look again. How about starting to de-cypher the hieroglyphics the Space Man left? Actually to look, to study, to understand. Have you *seen* a set? Why not write to 'Viewpoint Aquarius' (address at the end) and acquire a pair, left foot and right foot.

101

It may lead far.
The return arc of evolution back to One-ness IS,
Let's start now.


SECTION 5. *1947–54 More information*
If the previous two sections have been skipped, or even skimmed, then dear reader the path to studious research becomes unnecessarily inhibited.

Shelves full of books deal with the outer facts of this period of seven years of open discussion, and amply will provide proofs to all who care to examine. A brief summary, with huge gaps, is all that can be given here. But did you know?

*Norwegian Government film*
1. The Norwegian government filmed two Saucers on colour film.

Wanting to record a particular eclipse of the sun in early 1954 they sent up three aircraft, packed full of sophisticated equipment, with 50 hand-picked scientists aboard; even the glass had been altered in the portholes to minimise refraction of light.

While descending after their mission was completed, while still at 10,000 feet, all three separate aircraft, with 50 scientists aboard, all saw two Saucers, 'silver-metallic, manoeuvring'.

The chief cameraman hurriedly unpacked his equipment and managed to take a ten-second colour film of them. In a ten-second sequence there are a very large number of separated 'frames'; all showed 'two saucers, silver-metallic, manoeuvring'.

Can you honestly imagine such a film, taken in those circumstances, with 50 witnesses of that calibre, being faked?

*Crashed Saucers captured*
2. Crashed Saucers have been captured. Did you know? For example:
Spitzbergen 1952 – by the Norwegians.

Heligoland 1949 – by the British

New Mexico 1949 – the Americans gave a few details including that there were 16 bodies aboard of some 3 to 4 feet in height; that the (unknown) metal was impossible to cut; that the system of wires/tubes 'led no-where' in our nuts-and-bolts sense, but led directly to the etheric forces in an immensely powerful inner sense!

## Over Washington for Three nights

3. Demonstrations over large cities, with radar-fixes.

Washington D.C., July 1952. The most powerful of the earth cities was asleep; guarded by two civilian and one military radar installations. Sixteen saucers came overhead, into the forbidden air space right over the capital. All three radar installations tracked them, and could see them visually – a double lock of (triple) radar plus (triple) visual.

Fighters were scrambled, saw them visually and locked on with their radar.

A four-fold check of ground visual + radar, and air visual + radar.

The Saucers withdrew at an incredible speed; the fighters remained airborne patrols till fuel ran low, and landed. Instantly the Saucers returned, the fighters re-fuelled and gave chase;

again the four-fold lock of ground visual + radar, and air visual + radar,

again the Saucers withdrew, the fighters landed, the Saucers returned.

This went on all night! Hour after hour. The entire night.

And the next night.

And the night after that.

Three consecutive nights, so many hectic hours.

Imagine the furore, that did make headline news in the 1947–54 period of open discussion. *Life Magazine* (remember?) called it the greatest event since Jesus Christ.

But there was more to it than that. Sometimes the Saucers would be seen on radar (three separate ground installations; plus the separate airborne radar of the

individual jets of the Fighter Wing) but not visually;
    sometimes visually, by ground and by air, but not on radar;
    sometimes both, sometimes neither,
    sometimes flicking from radar to visual, and back.
    Repeatedly have Saucers shown this ability elsewhere too – to Capt. Howard of BOAC while flying the Atlantic on a scheduled flight, pacing the airliner for 21 (3 x 7) minutes and watched by the crew and passengers;
    this ability of being seen – being invisible; responding to radar, or not. At will.
    Also to change physical shape. At will. The nuts-and-bolts 'know' that solid matter doesn't change shape, that it either reflects radar or not; yet—
    the Saucers, the Initiates, the gods, all demonstrate that the control of the six inner bodies can make the outer physical one not only change shape, be visible or not, but be heavy (Adamski contact) be light (Medina contact), and much much more. It's time to learn!
    Let's start now.

*Eight Governments*
    4. By now the government of Venezuela, the government of Argentina, the government of Mexico had all come out publicly in their belief in the reality of Flying Saucers, and had published their photographs, their films, the reports of their armed forces personnel, details of demonstrations over their cities, of the landings even.
    The government of Brazil did it this way: on 2 December, 1954 its chief of Air Staff called a press conference and released whole pages of photographs/films/facts, substantiated and documented in technical detail. The Brazilian newspapers published full-page colour supplements to carry the news. By now the clamp-down of 1954, which is our next section below, had become operative and not a word, not a photo was published in England or in America. Why?
    On 18 January, 1958 the Brazilian President himself, as distinct from the Chief of Air Staff, again called a press conference and again released more facts/films/radar/

104

technical data, reiterating that Flying Saucers were real.

Not a word was, or since has, been published in the UK or the USA. Why?

The Norwegian government has followed suit. Not reported by the UK and the USA. Why?

So too, in 1962, did the Swedish government (page 108)

and the government of the Philippines.

Why don't we, now, years later, publish these facts/photos/films?

Why the silence?

The government of Chile released a long official colour film of groups of saucers hovering over Antarctica, as taken by a naval vessel. Would you not like to see it? Be allowed to!

The evidence piles high.

But it's time to discuss how/why the fierce censorship came to be imposed.


Section 6. *USA Government contact 1954 with Saucers*

Strenuously it has been denied, ever since. Scorn, ridicule pour on those who insist that it was so; rigid enforcement of official secrets-acts blankets the many who know. Too many, because the whispers slip out, persistently, and build a consistent picture, which becomes ever clearer.

First, and undeniably obvious, is the plain fact which anyone can verify by research in reference libraries: before 1954, for seven years, the news media reported Saucers;

in 1954 the censorship cut off the news – at the stroke of a knife;

not only for the USA and its allies, but for Russia and China as well.

That fact is true. Is clear. How do you explain it? In 1954 the cold war was on, Stalin had died, the Berlin blockade still wrankled, everyone was pointing guns at everyone else; can you think of any other major international event which has Russia, China, America,

England, Europe, Africa, Asia all in total agreement?!

It's unbelievable – but provable.

Five Flying Saucers, of different types (sixteen distinct types have been catalogued) landed at Muroc; at Edwards Air Force base; by prior arrangement; stayed forty-eight hours; and were inspected by the top political, military and scientific brass, who also were taken for rides.

What a mouthful of a sentence! No wonder it is almost impossible to credit. Yet please consider:

Given the situation of Saucer demonstrations all over the planet, of the hundreds upon thousands of reports, of the governments who published convincing proofs, of the millions of folks who had seen, of the thousands who had contacted;

what, then, was strange in an approach being made to the USA? *Life Magazine* had already described the three consecutive nights over Washington D.C. as the greatest event since Jesus Christ, and that was already a full two years ago during which the reports had mounted;

the Canadian Government in 1949 had set up an official enquiry, under Wilbur Smith, head of the Telecommunications Project, and had reported Saucers to be real;

it had become too big for Canada, and the USA set up Project Grudge 1950 to investigate, quickly enlarging it to Project Twinkle;

by 1955 every major government had installed full-blown (secret) departments to investigate, and all had reported confidentially that Saucers were real, 'incredible reports from credible witnesses' was the American conclusion. Please don't confuse this with the outer (and quite well known) departments, whom you could phone, who would listen courteously to your sighting, and gravely explain it away with jargonese.

*Official Government Investigations*

As early as 1957 serious researchers got to know of these inner, and very very powerful, departments, and we published the following details:

106

*Canada* Telecommunications Special Project of December 1949, became Project Magnet under Wilbur Smith. When he personally made contact with Saucers, became convinced they were benevolent, released information including how to make a simple instrument (details are available) for detecting and for measuring 'magnetic anomolies' – which cause landslips, holes in the ground while 'ranging downwards', and aircraft crashes when 'ranging upwards' – anomalies engendered as a totally unforeseen side effect of nuclear explosions then being carried out by the Super Powers, Wilbur Smith was sacked as 'unstable'. Never again was he given a responsible post.

January 1952, Defence Research Board Project was set up.

*France* General Staff Committee, spring 1955, enlarging and replacing the Research Committee of July 1952.

*Great Britain* Deputy Director of Intelligence Air Ministry 1952. [We are prevented from giving the exact title of the department, the name and rank of the official in charge – although all that is known.]

In 1959 the author persuaded a National British Newspaper Editor to test the theory of an inner and high-ranking department. 1959 was the time of silence / ridicule stages – as detailed below. Without actually going so far as to say so, this newspaper published a long article suggesting the existence of such a department; drew a line of dots; and below that published the photograph of a very famous name of the Armed Forces, then the technical Head of this department; also, it witnessed / heard the author phone the (secret) telephone number, give his name and qualifications as a Flying Saucer researcher and ask to report some questions; there was a shocked silence at the other end of the telephone; a smooth delaying action. When we rang back in two hours – the telephone number had been changed and that line was 'not in use'.

*Italy* UFO Investigating Committee, July 1954.

*Yugoslavia,* Board of Enquiry, December 1954.
The author was visited in London, some years later, still within the silence / ridicule stages, by the son of the current Foreign Minister for Yugoslavia, who not only confirmed the existence of this Board, its date of origin, but offered information; Yugoslavia was on the point of following the example of other governments – eight in all – and of openly admitting the reality of Saucers; financial loans / pressure seemed to have caused a change of mind. This government, like all others, had its own convincing proofs / photos / landings of Saucers.

*Norway* Research Committee, February 1956.

*Sweden* Defence Committee, Research Project. On 28 June, 1962 the Commander-in-Chief of the Swedish forces publicly handed over the official files on Saucers, the complete list of sightings filed by the Ministry of Defence to Professor Troeng, Chairman of the Swedish Unidentified Flying Objects Research Society.

*USA* Project Blue Book (Major Charles Harding, officer i / c). 4602 Air Intelligence Squadron investigate all reported sightings.
This 4602 Squadron was in existence until at least the late 1960s, one of its Wing Commanders came out in favour of Saucers, and admitted personal contact with them, (a contact that he had passed on to higher echelons) immediately after the elapse of the ten-year official secrets silence gap on technical information after his retirement. At once, after his 'leak of information' – ten years after retirement – he ceased to talk any more about it.
Please consider the cost of maintaining a whole squadron; it puts into perspective the much publicized trifle of $300,000 for the Condor Report – a futile attempt at denying the reality of Saucers, 1969.
The forty-eight questions, on a four-page questionnaire sent to all Service personnel by this squadron, if a Saucer

sighting/landing was witnessed, was currently in use at least till 1970.

Particularly detailed were the instructions for noting the presence and behaviour by snails, slugs, moluscs in the landing area, because their behaviour gave important clues to radiation fields and their strength. Insistent were the instructions that special helicopters, equipped with very sophisticated infra-red cameras, were to photograph the site/moluscs from specified heights/directions. The 4602 squadron being available on permanent stand-by duty.

*USSR* Research Committee of Dept. of Defence, set up April 1955.

With such a background, a mere fraction of the facts which researchers have been able to glean, but which are thought-provoking in the extreme, and of a consistency lasting *and increasing* year by year, let us now look at the contact of the US Government.

*Muroc, Edwards Air Force Base, contact spring 1954*

The five different types of Saucers landed, by prior arrangement, stayed forty-eight hours, were examined by the top military/scientific/political authorities, gave rides, and demonstrated:

ability to become visible – invisible

transparent-walk through – dense solid;

expand to very large – shrink to very small (while staying stationary on the ground)

vertical take-offs/landings – in silence,

reflect radar – or not

Speeds/manoeuvrability – out of this world, and in such silence;

even 'the air did not get displaced' so that no sonic booms

result. Incredible.

But all, all, understandable and explainable and realizable when the Occult section at the beginning of the book is considered.

But, all this put our nuts-and-bolts earthling science well and truly in the shade;

109

worse still, to duplicate it, required the unheard of
qualification of – unselfishness of motive. Such a ridiculous
pre-requisite. Yet so very easily seen to be essential if
what this book outlines of the inner planes, of the Law
of Karma (of Cause and Effect), of Balance, of Justice
– is even remotely accurate.

Whoever heard of an earthling government being
unselfish – enlightened self-interest being the best available,
that is, clever and more far-seeing selfishness; disguised,
made palatable.

Whoever heard of an earthling being unselfish? That
was the job of 'gods'. It certainly is the hall-mark of the
Golden Thread of Beings of the return arc of evolution
back to One-ness; it certainly is the goal for humanity,
who certainly are striving; are succeeding in greater or
lesser part; with many lapses – who yet progress, who yet
see Saucers, and make contact.

As did the government at Muroc:

*Straws-in-the-wind / Proof?*

The President of the USA suddenly leaves 'on a golfing
holiday'; to Palm Springs; which is near the Air Force
Base. His valet lets slip that the President forgot to take
his golf clubs with him.

Large numbers of Base personnel, away on routine jobs
or passes suddenly found re-entry barred for forty-eight
hours. But barred. Equally no one, but no one, emerged
out for forty-eight hours.

Far too many personnel actually saw the Saucers; many
heard the top brass animatedly / dis-orientatedly discussing
them, and the examination of their interior cabins and
layouts – and of the rides in them.

Saucers could be seen – not heard – taking off and
landing.

These sort of stories from little people, in increasingly
louder whispers are multifold – consistent to a degree.

The 1954 censorship in Russia, China, Amercia,
England, and other countries is *provable.*

One eye-witness report has slipped out of the hush-hush
bag; it was sent to Z, one of the best of the Saucer

researchers at the time:

*From:* [The Name, and even the address, had been
written – but deemed prudent now to erase]
*dated* 16.4.54.

To: Mr. Z of San Diego, California (we had to suppress
this!)

'My dear friend,

I have just returned from Muroc. The report is true . . .
devastatingly true! I made the journey with (erased) of
the . . . Papers, and (erased) Institute (Truman's erstwhile
advisor) and Bishop (erased) (confidential names for the
present, please).

'When we were allowed to enter the restricted section
(after about six hours in which we were checked on every
possible item, event, incident and aspect of our personal
and public lives), I had the distinct feeling that the world
had come to an end with fantastic realism. For I have
never seen so many human beings in a state of complete
collapse and confusion as they realized that their own
world had indeed ended with such finality as to beggar
description. The reality of 'other plane' aeroforms is now
and forever removed from the realms of speculation and
made a rather painful part of the consciousness of every
responsible scientific and political group.

'During my two days' visit, I saw five separate and
distinct types of aircraft being studied and handled by
our airforce officials . . . with assistance and permission
of the Etherians – I have no word to express my reactions.

'It has finally happened. It is now a matter of history'.

'President Eisenhower, as you may already know, was
spirited over to Muroc one night during his visit to
Palm Springs recently. And it is my conviction that he
will ignore the terrific conflict between the various
"authorities" and go directly to the people via radio and
television – if the impasse continues much longer. From
what I could gather, an official statement to the country
is being prepared for delivery about the middle of May'.

'I will leave it to your excellent powers of deduction
to construct a fitting picture of the mental and emotional
pandemonium that is now shattering the consciousness of

111

hundreds of our scientific "authorities" and all the
pundits of the various specialized knowledges that make
up our current physics. In some instances I could not
stifle a wave of pity that arose in my own being as I
watched the pathetic bewilderment of rather brilliant brains
struggling to make some sort of rational explanation
which would enable them to retain their familiar theories
and concepts. And I thanked my own destiny for having
long ago pushed me into the metaphysical woods and
compelled me to find my way out. To watch strong minds
cringe before totally irreconcilable aspects of "science"
is not a pleasant thing. I had forgotten how
commonplace such things as the dematerialization of
"solid" objects had become to my mind. The coming and
going of an etheric or spirit body had been so familiar
to me these many years that I had just forgotten that
such a manifestation could snap the mental balance of a
man not so conditioned. I shall never forget those 48
hours at Muroc.'

Now substantiation from:

*Senator Barry Goldwater,* retired Air-Force Brigadier
General, 1964 Republican Official Nominee for office of
President of the United States—
    who believes in Flying Saucers, has had forty-four years
of flying himself, who has personally had radio signals
from outer space: 'I've doubted stories from many
witnesses, but when qualified pilots and other experts
tell me they've seen strange, unexplained flying objects,
I have to put faith in their reports. Air Force, Navy and
commercial pilots have revealed to me cases where a
UFO would fly near them – right off their plane's wing
– and then just zoom away at incredible speeds';
    he says this of his attempt, with his record – Air Force,
and Republican nominee for the Presidency itself – of
trying to find out what happened (above) at Muroc:
    years and years later, 16 December, 1973: 'I've never
been able to get into the Air Force Research Office at
Wright-Patterson (Air Force Base where the central
(secret) files on Flying Saucers are Priority One, Top

112

Secret). I asked General Curtis LeMay, who for years was
the head of Strategic Air Command, for permission to
check into the files and he told me, "Hell, no, and don't
ask me again".'

Senator Goldwater re-iterated his views on 6 January,
1974: 'I believe the earth has been visited many times
by creatures from outer space . . . I can't believe that in
this never-ending universe our planet is the only one with
intelligent life. I'm not convinced that human beings are
the smartest creatures in the universe. I certainly believe
in aliens in space. They may not look or talk like us,
but I have very strong feelings that they have advanced
past our mental capabilities.'

That's precisely what the Muroc landing proved 'that
they have advanced past our mental capabilities'! And
that from a man who ran for President – but was still not
allowed to see the (secret) files.

Flying Saucers are very serious business indeed – long
advanced, far far past, our mental capabilities. But, we
are invited to catch up.


SECTION 7 *Silence – Why?*

Z's forecast that President Eisenhower would tell the
people proved wrong; as was thwarted even Senator
Goldwater's attempt nineteen years later to see the files.
Incidentally both President Eisenhower, and President
Lyndon Johnson had publicly announced, before their
election to the Presidency, to 'blow the lid off this Saucer
business'. Once in office – silence.

Why? Why not tell us?

Well let's think it out. All governments are selfish, as
are their peoples; so what do you do about a vastly more
superior – technologically, militarily, and morally – occult-
sort-of-visitor who insists that One-ness replaces
separateness? Would the Western rich-man fully share
with the African bush-man?

Every single thing of our lives is affected by Saucers:

(1) *Politics*

USA/England/Russia are strong, in part because they have energy (oil shortage notwithstanding!) of electricity, coal, hydro-electric works, oil, nuclear power.

Saucers use/need none of these. Using 'free energy from the air' – etheric inwards.

So what do you do with that (dumped) military + economic power?

What do you do with the jobs of those vast multitudes, their skills, their dividends, their investment, their salaries, their profits – the very sinews of the industrial set up? You could have an adult education programme in new skills, (force) move labour, re-adapt, etc., but the prime requirement is that you, and your people, be unselfish! How do you create/explain/manifest that?

(2) *'God'/Spiritual/Ethics*

The ethics part is universal, it seems, but what of all the other particularized title-holders of 'Up There'? Especially of those densified into an earthling 'He'? Do we seriously expect the huge variations in Life, in Intelligence, in Attributes-far-beyond-our-own, scattered through more habitable planets than we have houses, do we expect them all to come down to the dense level of our He-gods? To have funny little earthling bodies? What happens to all those special earthling people, 'chosen people', who claim the selfish privileges they do?

It makes you think! Especially if you've got a fancy title, fancy place, huge patronage/power/adulation with privileged priests/hierophants/califs feeding off the flocks. All those golden ornaments, silken clothes, horded treasures.

What happens to that lot if – unselfish – Saucers get to the multitudes?

(3) *Security*

What happens to all that gold-braid, those stripes/stars (Russian Red or American White) as you guard your territory in good old earthling separateness – and find yourself puny and helpless in the face of Saucers. And

114

are seen to be such.

What happens then?

(4) *Science*

A sort of lord of (physical) creation up to now. Everyone claps you as you pontificate. What happens to you when faced with time-travel, levitation, appear-disappear and the rest?

What happens to all your years of training, your medals, your degrees?

These questions begin to make you think when you start to get around to it – as the US government did at Muroc.

It affects the very essence of all our lives, at every level.

Flying Saucers are very serious business indeed.

So too is Truth / One-ness; more so than Power.

It's time to realize that. But it has to be done by each and all of us, individually in our millions; it can't really be imposed from above – after all Jesus was not born Caesar at Rome, the futility of that is obvious, you just can't make, by force, a man 'love his neighbour', be unselfish.

On our own two flat feet, by our own (hard) effort we have got, by ourselves, to get round the turning point from the downward into selfish matter arc, back up the return into One-ness path.

No–one / no-thing / no-system can do it for you, but you.

Let's start now.


SECTION 8. *Ridicule / Conventional Explanations*

Over the heads of governments – especially the most powerful ones with most to lose – the Flying Saucers began appealing to the multitudes for the next twenty years:

with the 'authorities' fighting a rear-guard action, losing all the time, getting more and more ridiculous in their brush-offs / their explanations / their denials;

we have all seen it;

some have refused to learn – and stayed blinded by fear;

but most have come around to truth. The Opinion
Polls verify that two out of three accept.

After all, the majority of us are self-conscious about
being selfish, are genuinely anxious to improve, are
striving to turn past the down-turn to the return arc.

Only the laggards resist; unavailingly; and, as already
said, their common characteristic? The over use of those
bitterly selfish words 'I' 'me' 'myself' 'personally'.

Do we really need more facts than that.

(For those who do – several hundred books on Saucers
will elaborate the 'scientific' aspects, and their unfoldment.

Huge areas of investigation are having to be omitted,
but are covered in earlier books: where do Saucers come
from, how many types, why don't they land in Hyde
Park, come on TV, what do they look like, what language
do they speak, are they all as advanced, what about
the humanoids, the unmanned Saucers, names and details
of the contactees, scientific proofs, verifiable with nuts-
and-bolts, etc. Except for the first question which is
considered in the next chapter, the reader is left now –
more than a quarter of a century later – to do some
catching up on his own.)


SECTION 9. *Alleged hostility*

The more imposing the spokesman, the more glossy
the magazine, the more established the pundit:

that is, the more the laggard with most at stake,

the more the denunciation of Saucers, ever since 1965,
and the more persistent the drumbeat alleging kidnapping/
abducting/ hynoptizing/manipulating by the naughty
naughty Saucers. Big Brother uniting with Big Daddy
to protect you – against THEM.

But the people have not been fooled. Those thousands
who've had contact know, for certain, Saucers to be
advanced spiritually as well as technically; to be patient;
they've been here since 18,000,000 B.C. waiting for us
to grow up;

others who have had sightings – and that runs into
hundreds of millions of ordinary decent folk – note that

the drumbeat of alleged hostility did not start till the cover-up of silence + ridicule + conventional explanations began to fail;

that the most shrill were those of the establishment, with a lot to lose;

also noticed that events that had passed serenely and objectively by, suddenly began to be revived as hostile after the mid 1960s when the cover-up collapsed.

It has not duped many. Let's hope it did not blind you. One-ness IS.

# 8. Venus/Angel Hair

SECTION 1. *Venusians*

That word has become well known, and actively attacked as unscientific, the nuts-and-bolts claiming to 'know' that no life is possible there;

the same experts also 'know' that solid matter does not change shape – as those ridiculous Flying Saucers keep proving to the contrary, and keep having to be brushed off as 'scientific irregularities';

yet instantaneous time-travel is done by these pain-in-our-official-neck Saucers, who just don't grub around with light years;

they even have the cheek of pre-cognition, mind reading, materialization, and other such 'unproven' stuff.

So irritating to the orthodox. It makes one think! Makes one re-orient! True the giants of science and the Nobel Peace prize-winners have done so (page 17) but it does make things so unshaky for us 'experts' (us second-raters/us cling-ons to our prejudice).

Not being stuck solidly in the seventh, and lowest, body – the dense physical – the Venusians live quite happily, it seems, focused as they are in the inner planes where the nuts + bolts arguments of what constitutes (physical) life and its environment leave them serenely unconcerned.

Anyway, how does humanity know that Venusians

exist? Because the Space Travellers say so. The recognized
experts don't / can't make contact themselves and merely
snort and sniff when thousands do. The earthling always
seems to ask two questions of the Space People, and
frequently in the order as now put:

(1) *Why contact me, a nobody, why not go to (some
authoritative symbol)?*
 The answer to that is crucial, and has been discussed
already; 'we don't choose you, you choose us'; an answer
that makes the tame expert hopping mad.

(2) *Where do you come from?*
 Venus, is the usual reply although there are at least
four main streams of Space Travellers – as discussed in
earlier books, like Flying Saucer Message.
 So why Venus,
 and what-do-they-look-like, what-language-do-they speak.
-

SECTION 2. *Why Venus?*
 In Part I of this book we took together a peep outside
this village of ours, planet earth, on a time scale of a
manvantara (technical term) of 4,320,000,000 year span
in seven great Root Races each developing one sense
(two are yet to come) and on a sevenfold level of the seven
'bodies' – the physical, the etheric, the desire-mind (Kama-
Manas), the Life Forces (Prana), and the inner triad of
full Mind (Manas), Love-Wisdom (Buddhi) and supreme
(Atma). It gave an altogether more enlarged viewpoint.
 So, if all is sevenfold, it does not now become too
unreasonable to consider that Life itself could have seven
great streams for our local little solar system and galaxy
– a tiny fragment of the whole. This sevenfold Life
Stream would have us earthlings, as one of the seven,
with others (perhaps more, or even less, advanced than
us mere five-sensers). The full story, in great technical
detail and cross-linked elaboration, is in the magnificent
work *The Secret Doctrine* of the great H. P. Blavatsky –
her compliment being that the petty / prejudiced /

encrusted, who have not seriously penetrated her writings, have denounced her as charlatan; the unjust fate, it seems, of the 'Golden Thread' of advanced Teachers – and the earnest researcher will find his questions, particularly the deeply thoughtful, illuminated therein.

Suffice for our present study the fact that of the sevenfold Life Stream it is the Venusians that have got themselves stuck with the lousy job of helping us quarrelsome/cocky little earthlings.

because the Venusians have already developed fully the quality of Mind (Manas) which is our next stage in the great class-room of Life, or as 'our books' hint – in my Father's house are many mansions.

It is they who have maintained, and still do maintain, a surveillance, a guard, a guide of Elder Brethren for these past Millions of years. Nuts-and-bolts screams about 'random probability' not being inducive of frequent space probes/contacts completely ignores the factor of Will – the Venusians are doing voluntary social work helping us delinquents to help ourselves, till one day we shall be worthy (and peaceful!) members of the Space family;

Venusian mind, Space mind, full Manas has a vast/ deep range (pp. 42/3) far far beyond our mental capabilities to re-quote Senator Barry Goldwater. One simple characteristic as stated was that without going into the library to have physically to handle a book, a Venusian mind would (a) know what was in the book, fully/ accurately (b) what was in the mind of the author when he wrote it (c) what was in the minds that influenced the mind of the author – all known instantaneously.

Hence, such Peoples 'and their Father are One'; 'in as much as a sparrow should fall'/'if these, the least of the brethren' – all would be known. Instantly. Fully. Accurately.

Mere mind reading becomes toy play by comparison.

It is the stage we earthlings will all have brought to fruition in our Sixth Root Race, in our Sixth body of Love-Wisdom (Buddhi) in time hence. Much time hence. But the rudiments are here, and millions of us glimmer and even flash; albeit spasmodically.

Meanwhile, since 18,000,000 B.C. when we started grappling with mind, the Venusians wait; and help us help ourselves. By the Laws of Balance/Justice/Karma – as ye sow thus shall ye reap – they are not allowed to do the irksome job for us. What good would that be? What good would it be for a Jesus to be born Caesar in Rome?

On our own two flat feet we have, each single unique one of us, to do it ourselves. When finally we have developed our earth mind to full Manas, Space Mind, by the full fusion of our good concrete mind (chewing gum/ bombs and all) with the deep metaphysical mind of the Aryan Root Stock, first sub root of our Fifth Root Race (poverty, gurus, and all) then we earthlings will have our own unqiue contribution to make to the Sevenfold Life Stream – stability.

The cussedness of the ears-back donkey that we all have, will be transmuted to the four-fold strength of fire/ air/water/earth legs, plus the permeability of the whole as we all then have the strength to stride forth.

We shall indeed then ride through Jerusalem on an ass (ourselves, by ourselves, by our own effort).

But signs in the sky abound; they have never been lacking. The foolish scoff; the wiser investigate – and grow. Much progress has been made since the Third Root Race (touch + hearing + sight) of Lemuria, now below the Pacific, 18 to 5 million B.C.; since the Fourth Root Race (touch + hearing + sight + taste) of Atlantis, 4 million to 1 million B.C.; and now in the Fifth Root Race, one million years old, with smell added to our faculties. More progress awaits the aware.

Remember the many stories of the fantastically high speeds of the Venusians? Zooming off in their Saucers; running in front of police cars so fast that the car could not catch up; working in a printers' shop and type-setting so fast that the other operatives were dumbfounded? (details in earlier books). If all we mouthed was an excuse not to look – hallucination, schizophrenic, etc. – we stayed stuck in our rut; but serious researchers began to realize the infinitely quicker speeds of the mental planes (sevenfold) and how a true focus in the highest

121

could cause to move / vibrate the dense physical at an
unbelievable rate, e.g. to run on 2 separate earthling-
type legs, with an earthling type body, so fast along the
road that a police car could not keep pace. Remember
those old old myths of seven leagued boots flashing
across country?!

Venusians themselves glide / permeate, or dematerialize /
re-materialize from 'here' to 'there' instantly, e.g. (*a*) in
time – so that they can travel from past, present, future,
at will, and positively are not stuck in a flat linear
pastpresentfuture rut. (*b*) in space so that they can get
from 'Venus' to 'here' with the speed of thought, and
make those famous 186,000 miles per second of the
nuts-and-bolts look like the grubs they are. Instantaneous
space travel makes nonsense of light-years. (*c*) they can
'come' can 'materialize' can 'register on radar', instantly,
be it in the Pentagon / Kremlin / Cabinet Room – or not.
At will. No wonder they're so difficult to capture!
Remember all those stories of Saucers, Space Peoples,
Lights that are there / and are not – in the instant of time.
Jibing at the stories leads one way; examining, and
hence realizing the potentialities of the powers of Manas
(full Mind) leads another. Remember all those old old
myths of 'invisible people'? Remember all those Saucer
stories when the photographs taken of them by earthlings
showed (1) either the visible Saucer reproduced on the
photo, plus an occupant who had remained invisible to
the earthling range of the physical eye, or (2) of not coming
out on the photo, or (3) of something different coming out.
Screaming fake / fraud was one way; another was to realize
the powers of materialize – dematerialize that control
of Manas gives.

All this requires ordered progression, under Law, in
due proportion to *right* effort, *right* motive. There are
no short cuts, special stooges who'll do the job for us,
Saviours or whatever.

Meditation. Occult. Yoga. These are big big words.
Let's start now.

Meanwhile the Venusians take the shape / body we want
or we expect. They talk the language we understand,

be it mere word-noises we call 'language' or be it inner /
truer / accurate / instantaneous communication, of
whatever level the earthling can reach. 'To a child I
"speak" as a child.'

We earthlings have much to learn; our potentiality is
enormous; we too can be Space Peoples – after all, we
already live on a Space Ship, planet earth – and we have
every inducement, every example, every sign in the
Sky that we need to make ourselves, by ourselves, grow.
Let's start now.


Section 3. *'People of the Web'. Angel Hair*
Two out of three accept the reality of Flying Saucers,
so the 'need for proof' stage has passed; it is only the
minority of laggards that still argue, but the rest of us
are moving on to further stages;

some are getting frightened of them. Any tame
psychologist will tell you of our earth tendency to
project on to others our own hidden fears; it is still those
on the downward arc-into-matter, motivated by fear and
hence separateness, who most accuse the Saucers of alleged
hostility – the reversal of the Truth; in the name of
Reason what would the full Mind, Manas, of a Venusian
want by way of conquest! They've been patiently stuck
with us lot since Lemuria;

but most are beginning to investigate, thrilled in a
tentative way, of becoming Space Peoples ourselves, as
we edge our way round the turning point back along the
return arc of One-ness.

Who not-so-much-take, as seek to be in Wholeness;
who not-so-much-separate-off as seek the Wholeness of
Understanding – both of their fellow creatures (mineral,
vegetable, animal, man, Space Man) and of the very
throb of the Universe itself – pure motion (not e-motion),
touched / sensed / sought at the Lipika Webs, which
sub-stand 'substance'.

Such are known as 'People of the Web'.

Their links are subtle to a degree – but strong, are
recognizable, are real, are utterly impossible to fake –

123

or to miss. 'People of the Web' always sense other 'People of the Web'.

Their joint keynote – 'touching' the throb of the Inmost Itself – easily leads to a new way of Life, to the New Age of Aquarius, to care for All, to telepathy, to powers of the mind, to all that Clairvoyance – Clairaudience – Clairsentience ARE.

In all its multifold facets, in all its multilevelled ways – the visible and the invisible, the temporal and the spiritual, with a strong overtone of concentric group, of unity, of One-ness.

Such people often make Flying Saucer Contacts.

Such people often find Angel Hair. It looks like a spider's web, but is not; it seems of little importance, but is not. The four elements of the 'old age' (be it Pisces, or far far older as we have already detailed) had the four elements of fire, air, water, earth; the fifth element is already manifesting – as H. P. Blavatsky wrote in her stupendous *Secret Doctrine* and called it 'permeability'. Unifying, permeating brick walls so that you can see through; prejudices so that unity is; restrictions so that humanity's potentialities are; the power of thought (Manas) on a Space scale replacing the physical motivations of nuclear power, coal, oil, etc; the end of the 18,000,000 years of quarantine as full-Manas Man rejoins his Space Brothers in One-ness.

Of Angel Hair, beloved by 'People of the Web', the magazine *Viewpoint Aquarius* said in its No. 8 issue:

'So often found in conjunction with Flying Saucers; so often glibly dismissed as spider's webs, as unimportant.'

Has it a significance?

Maddening are the qualities of Angel Hair: you can't force it to come; when it does you can't keep it, make it return again – in the same place, let alone to a chosen person – you can't intrigue it to appear/stay; you can't bargain/trick/compromise; it cares not a fig for powerful people/authoritative people/experts/hydrogen bombs/or all the other dense physical stuff that dominates earthlings.

Angel Hair seems to respond to thoughts, pure/ wholesome/unselfish thoughts; to the quality of the aura. Lose that quality even for a day – and Angel Hair vanishes. It seems to re-appear only and solely when the 'balance' has been restored.

Just like Flying Saucers themselves! No wonder the powerful/downward arc/basically selfish/men of physical authority dismiss or decry it – as they do Flying Saucers.

Yet; Angel Hair forms, frequently, repeatedly, and all over this village, planet earth, and has done ever since the dawn of time.

Many many people find it; often; as they do Flying Saucers – only to be shrugged off by the dense-physically orientated as fools/liars/psychics/hallucinated.

Do you see it? Do you believe that trained and focused thoughts can control/affect/change the weather – or are you content with seeding rain clouds by aeroplanes? Do you really believe/know/strive for One-ness – or will the Quantum Theory of dense-only physics suffice?'

Well?

It's a choice. And to be made.

If you actively are seeking Angel Hair, this is often found in company with 'Mother Nature', with grass and trees, or with open waters and seas; it seems to need earthling co-operation and gets inhibited by overwhelming hostile thoughts, although not prevented. Sceptics dismiss it as spiders' webs. Of a white colour that includes all colours, it has a beautiful linear pattern – symbolic to some of the razor-edged path – that vast link, joining all to Allness, at all levels, in all times, and in all ways, both of so-called good and for so-called evil, the hidden and the manifested. Superimposed on all this directional linear pattern is an even more encompassing concentric pattern/rhythm, of meaning and beauty. The circular web. Touched with mineral or vegetable kingdom, the Angel Hair stays on – pick it up from the morning grass with a stone or a twig and it stays; touched by animal-man it melts, evaporates in the palm of the hand, but leaves no moisture or any physical trace behind. Animal-man is of the downward arc.

Permeability (the fifth element) is of its quality; evolutionary return upward arc is of its time; it is Flying Saucer linked; it is found / noticed by 'People of the Web'.
May you have luck / perseverance finding it.'
Let's start now.

# PART FIVE
## *LIVING VIEWS*

The Reader and the studious researcher will no doubt both agree that Life as outlined in this book, both in this planet and not, both in the physical and not, both in the visible and not, that such Life has many facets, many depths.

We each tend to strike only the area of our own particular occult sound, as yet; hence to be less-than-whole.

To help correct such imbalance, five earthlings now offer each their individual note, in the earnest hope that others may be helped thereby. It is not that a superior status is claimed, or anything ridiculous like that; merely that a persevering focus on these hidden rather than obvious, noumenon rather than phenomenon, cause rather than effect, views has been maintained for many a year and thus has permeated the occult sound.

Cordially are you invited to participate, in the five sounds of these five earnest seekers for Truth. Overlaps exist, to enrich, as all sample common areas of Life, yet each is refreshingly unique. The scope is so vast / deep that repetition is not only welcome but unifying.

# A concept of Mahatmas, Chelas [Self-disciplined disciple] and their Work
## by Olive Dutta

THE purpose of man's evolution on this planet is the attainment of Mahatmaship, that is, to transform ourselves as we are now – the very ordinary faulty human being – into perfected spiritually based man. The word Mahatma is the combination of two Sanskrit words, Maha – great, and atma – soul. This interpreted correctly means a human being whose whole focus when working on this planet is centred in the highest part of his constitution – his Higher Self or Spiritual Soul. These Mahatmas are called 'genius' and explaining the word literally but briefly means this:

1. Extraordinary intelligence surpassing that of most intellectually superior individuals.

2. Aptitude of doing or achieving some particular thing especially a gift or talent.

3. The essential or distinguishing characteristic of a particular individual.

4. A genius is sometimes described as a guide of a person throughout life. A good example of this being the 'genius' of Socrates.

All the above would correctly describe a Mahatma. These great Beings are our elder Brothers in point of evolution and spiritual relationship. That is, they help man, when ready for their guidance, on the path of evolution in a *spiritual* sense. Although it has been known that they work to this end through quite mundane agents, using those individuals capable of understanding through pure intellect their deep spiritual teachings, a greater part of their work consists of watching over, and stimulating *spiritually*, on an inner level, the life of the human race.

The Mahatma's knowledge is founded upon *experience,* something which he actually *knows* – – – this being a *working* knowledge of all Nature, create and uncreate, and of *self* directed evolution. He is the perfection of the great human development scheme of our planet.

We understand the Mahatmas to be a great Brotherhood which has existed from the very earliest days of humanity, when at long last *self*-consciousness was awakened in the souls of man who then became aware of intellectual and emotional power and capable of love and hate. Having the power to choose, he created his own future and indeed his own *future self*. The desire for knowledge flowered in his now awakened mind. As the ages rolled by, the superhuman Instructors of the race of man, called in esoteric teachings, Manasaputras (technical term – developers of earthling mind attribute), were succeeded by their Chelas or Disciples, the Mahatmas. And so from the very early days, there has been an organization of advanced beings who supervised the progress of humanity. *And they exist still today.*

In these very early days the Mahatmas lived openly among men, and they were understood as Teachers, and were listened to and obeyed. But there comes a time when an infant grows to adolescence, and wishes to do things his own way. Man then became immensely selfish, wilful and grasping, more and more materialistic, and blind to the deep spiritual teachings given out by their elder brothers. This very dense state in the evolution of man is described in Vol. II of *The Secret Doctrine* by H. P. Blavatsky as the Atlantean period for which we are still suffering and reaping the effects of the causes laid down in that great but eventually decadent civilization. As indeed we are now making the effects which will be evident in time to come. So, sooner or later, the Mahatmas were no longer revered and looked to for teaching and inspiration by the majority of the people, and it was then that they retreated into silence and began their occult or hidden work in order to safeguard their secrets against exploitation and misuse.

They initiated special individuals and we understand that it was through their influence that the great Mystery Schools were formed. Quoting from *The Secret Doctrine,* Vol. II – 'All that is good, noble, and grand in the human nature, every divine faculty and aspiration, were cultivated by the Priest (Initiate Ed.) – Philosophers, who sought to develop them in their Initiates. Their code of ethics based on altruism, has become universal.'

We will now try to understand what actually goes to make a Mahatma. Two things are involved in the development of spiritual powers. First, a man must understand himself and this is no easy task when we realize that we are composed of seven parts, each one a living entity on its own. Then he must be able to comprehend the Universe in relation to himself. We all know the very ancient aphorism: 'Man know thyself, for within lie all the wisdom and potencies of the Universe'.

These are the first two steps on the path before attaining or even attempting chelaship. Man's knowledge of his own constitution, of his own capabilities and powers, is the key to unlock the first door of the world beyond the purely physical.

In H. P. Blavatsky's *Collected Writings,* she expounds on Self-knowledge, and a few of the rules can be mentioned here:

1. The first necessity for obtaining Self-knowledge is to become profoundly conscious of ignorance; to feel that one is ceaselessly self-deceived (the little i, or lower self is meant here).

2. The second is the still deeper conviction that such knowledge, such intuition which is *certain* knowledge, *can*

be obtained by effort.

3. Third, and most important, is the indomitable determination to obtain and *face* that knowledge.

This last is certainly very difficult.

In an adept or Mahatma the creative imagination that we use every day and the *spiritual* will of which we normally have little knowledge, will have been raised to their highest degree in the human development. The emphasis here is on the 'spiritual' will, for the personal or little will with its narrow viewpoint and its self-centred desire will not help the Mahatma in his work in the inner spiritual realms. The will must first be purified and made *im*personal. It must be motivated by altruism and universal charity. The Mahatma would have trained himself along these lines for many lives, although we understand from our teachings that strangely enough those latter lives in which an individual gains adeptship are not very numerous.

The fact is that the Adept, having allied himself with the Universal Soul of Nature, sometimes called Alaya or the Oversoul, in its many facets that is, physical, psychic, mental, psychological, spiritual – is able to stand at the apex of his own universe, as it were, and view the whole. He can see the *Causes* of human misery, and has the ability, within the great Law of Karma, to help. He has reached *Wisdom* in its truest sense, and can send spiritual power and energy into the thought atmosphere of the planet, causing many of the beneficent movements in history, and touching one or two individuals here and there who are ready for work of an altruistic nature for the benefit of humanity. In other words, those who are ready for the path of chelaship. The Blavatsky Teachings are one case in many; thinkers, scientists, philosophers, philantrophists will often respond to these spiritual currents which are sent out constantly by the Mahatmas who will encourage and inspire all who are advanced enough to feel them.

As these Mahatmas operate on an entirely different level from that of average humanity, it will be obvious that not many can respond to such high-powered thought. But

is we *ourselves* who choose to become chelas, the
Mahatmas do not choose us. As we are told in the
*Mahatma Letters to A. P. Sinnett* – 'Come out of your
world into ours'; and again 'If you really want to become
a chela, that is, to become a recipient of our mysteries,
*you* have to adapt yourself to *our* ways not we to yours.'
It is by our thought, word and deeds that we *force* the
Mahatmas to notice us, and that we have the opportunity
of becoming a chela.

There is an ancient saying that discipline precedes the
Mysteries, and we can understand why. For instance, to
be able to smash the atom and release such terrible forces,
with all the dangers which attend such power, gives an
idea of the potentiality for either good or evil which the
knowledge of *occult science* could bring which is so much
more powerful. So, necessarily, moral and spiritual
discipline of a most serious kind must precede the
student's chelaship.

The word Chela means a disciple or disciplined one,
who has offered himself or herself, as a pupil to learn
*practically,* not just know *about it,* the hidden mysteries
of Nature from a Mahatma or spiritual Teacher. Certain
rules have to have been complied with *before* being
accepted, and here are listed briefly just a few (from Book
4 of the *Collected Writings* of H. P. Blavatsky):

1. Perfect physical health.
2. Absolute mental and physical purity.
3. Unselfishness of purpose; universal charity; pity for all
animate beings.
4. Truthfulness and unswerving knowledge of the law
of Karma; independent of any power in nature that could
interfere; not to be caused to deviate by prayer or
propitiatory exoteric ceremonies.
5. A courage undaunted in every emergency, even by
peril to life.
6. An intuitional perception of one's being as the
vehicle of the manifested Atman (Supreme).
7. Calm indifference for, but a just appreciation of
everything that constitutes the objective transitory world,
in its relation with and to the invisible regions.

All these, except perhaps the first, i.e. perfect physical health, which in some cases has been known to have been modified, must have been more or less developed by the chela, *himself,* before being accepted by his Teacher.

The Mahatmas do *not* require a passive mind, they seek for those who are most active, who have logic and reasoning, for, as they say, they 'prefer people who can put two and two together once on the right scent'.

Intuition is a vital point, always remembering that intuition is *certain knowledge,* not merely a 'hunch'.

One of the main tests is the amount of dilligence and zeal that the neophyte puts into his work. He has to reach the condition necessary, i.e. the degree of illumination for which he is fitted before any occult secrets can be trusted to him.

Illumination must come from within, it is not enough to read about it, and no outside ritual of any kind can give it.

Fasting, meditation, chastity of thought, word and deed, silence for certain periods; government of natural passions and impulses, utter unselfishness of intention, and many other qualities must be complied with to suit the temperament of each chela and is watched over carefully by the Teacher.

To offer oneself as a candidate for chelaship is simple enough – to develop into a Mahatma is the most difficult thing a man could undertake – always remembering that he first has to be *accepted* as a chela, which is no easy task as we have seen.

The extremely long training and discipline undergone by him is vital if the forces he learns to control are not to be used for negative purposes. As the Mahatma says in one of his letters to Sinnett: 'I say again that it is he alone who has the love of humanity at heart who is capable of grasping thoroughly the idea of regenerating practical brotherhood who is entitled to the possession of our secrets . . .'

And if humanity ignores the teaching? Let us hear from the Mahatma himself:

' . . . We have offered to exhume the primeval state of Man's being, his basic nature, and lay bare the wonderful complications of his inner Self . . . It is our mission to plunge and bring the pearls of Truth to the surface; theirs (men of science) is to clean and set them into scientific jewels. And, if they refuse to touch the ill-shapen oyster-shell, insisting that there is not nor cannot be any precious pearl inside it, then we shall once more wash our hands of any responsibility before human-kind. For countless generations hath the Adept builded a fane of imperishable rocks, a giants Tower of Infinite thought wherein the Titan dwelt, and will yet, if need be, dwell alone, emerging from it but at the close of every cycle, to invite the elect of mankind to co-operate with him and help in his turn enlighten superstitious man. And we will go on in that periodical work of ours; we will not allow ourselves to be baffled in our philanthrophic attempts until that day when the foundations of a new continent of thought are so finely built that no amount of opposition and ignorant malice guided by the Brethren of the Shadow will be found to prevail.'

# Universal Law
## by Jean Coulsting

WHY do the stars not fall out of the sky? How do we
know that the seasons will follow one after the other in
regular succession? What makes it a certainty that the
sun will always appear in the East in the morning, and
disappear in the West in the evening? How is it possible
to predict the quarters of the moon and the times of its
rising? Why does an acorn always grow into an oak tree
and never anything else? Why are the colours of the
rainbow always in the same order? . . . The list of such
questions is endless. Does the answer lie in a Supreme
Being – a so-called 'god' of some kind who/which
personally decrees/directs that these things shall be –
and sees that they are? If that is the case, how come that
this same 'god' is able to be placated/propitiated/
pleaded with by mortal humans into altering the status
quo by granting favours to suit their personal whims and
fancies? Would this course of action not upset the finely
held balance of the Whole? Does it make sense?

Or is there another answer? – that the Universe is
sustained/stabilized by all-containing/all-pervading LAW
which is utterly impersonal, undeviating, but inexorably
just in maintaining all-inclusive harmony; LAW which
works through the Wholeness of manifestation/non-

manifestation, which 'deals' with the multitudinous millennia of individual parts as a totality in relationship to each other and thereby to One-ness; rather than as separate entities each pursuing its own self-seeking course? This, surely, does make sense.

So, the Universe operates according to Law, that is, in ordered patterns / processes which are predictable; nothing happens by chance or in a haphazard fashion under the dictates of a capricious 'god'. This is one of the most fundamental teachings of Occultism.

## I THE NATURE OF LAW

### 1. *Unity*

Law is Unity and Unity is Law. It is never 'created' by anyone / thing, for it always IS. In *The Secret Doctrine* by H. P. Blavatsky (Vol. I, p. 152) we read: 'It is idle to speak of "laws arising when Deity prepares to create" for (*a*) laws or rather LAW is eternal and uncreated, and (*b*) that Deity is Law and vice versa'. This means that Law still IS even in pralaya (the Cosmos in a state of rest / assimilation); it endures timelessly. 'Deity' here does not refer to a personal god, but rather is it equated with Space, which also is 'that which was, is and will be whether there is a Universe or not, whether there be gods or none' (*The Secret Doctrine*, Vol. I p. 9). LAW / SPACE is the Noumenon (the (hidden) cause; that which is subjective / within) from which emanates the whole of the phenomenal Universe, and equivalent terms variously used are BE-NESS, Universal Mind, the One homogeneous Substance-Principle. H. P. Blavatsky puts it thus (*The Secret Doctrine*, Vol. I p. 273) 'The fundamental Law in that system (that is, the Ageless Wisdom); the central point from which all emerged, around and toward which all gravitates, and upon which is hung the philosophy of the rest, is the One homogeneous divine SUBSTANCE-PRINCIPLE, the one radical cause.'

One SOURCE, One LIFE, One LAW – not three separate things, but tri-une UNITY.

## 2 *The One and the Many*

The ONE of the subjective state becomes the many of the objective universe; the Noumenon (unrevealed cause) gives rise to phenomena; the One Reality shows itself in various illusory forms. Thus, the ONE Law (which is uncreate, remember) manifests itself as a plurality of lesser laws, all inextricably interlinked and interwoven at every level of being because of their common link to The Source.

An illustrative analogy would be that of a rope, composed of many strands; each of the visible strands contains a lot of much smaller strands. The strength of the rope depends upon each of the parts acting in relationship to the whole, in their intertwined pattern. If the strands were used separately, or even together, but parallel to each other, the effectiveness of 'ropeness' would be entirely diminished. Or, we could think of a human physical body with all its different organs, limbs, nerves, blood system, etc. Each part has its own function to fulfil, not at the expense of all the others, but in unison with them. If any one part is 'out of order', the whole body suffers. So we see that the physical vehicle is not a mere aggregate of various bits and pieces (a union) but an epitome of Unity/Wholeness.

It is thus with Universal LAW, whose basic inherent quality is Unity/One-ness/Balance. As with the organs/parts of the body, each manifested law has its own function to perform, its own ring-pass-not; it cannot act in any other way than that decreed by the overall Law (the heart could not suddenly take over the duties of the liver) – yet – the total pattern is Harmony/Wholeness. Further, every manifested entity, from the greatest to the smallest, the highest to the lowest exists within the limits of some aspect of the Law. *Nothing* can possibly be outside it.

Therefore there is no such thing as 'supernatural' or beyond Nature. Supernormal there may be, that is, beyond the average which can be attained by most of humanity at present, but Supernatural – no! – for that would mean that phenomena not within the realms of Natural Law could occur, and that is obviously nonsense. What those who use the term do mean is that *events not explainable by present-*

*day science* take place. But, at long, long last, as we move forward, the break-through seems to be approaching. Scientists are *having* to admit that E.S.P./acupuncture/ 'faith' healing/astrology/etc. *do* work; that there are other planes/forces/laws in Nature besides the physical and what can be measured with/by physical instruments. Physics/science is having to give way to metaphysics/ Occult science – 'Occult' means hidden: the laws of gravity, electricity, magnetism, heat, etc., were all 'occult' before being 'discovered' by men. Why do we suppose that the science of the twentieth century has reached the ultimate and that what cannot be explained by it cannot exist/happen? – that there is no more for science to discover/unveil? What arrogance/conceit/stupidity!!

However – the 'break-through' has been coming for some time now with programmes on radio and television, articles/features in newspapers and magazines, and books; it seems to have been hastened tremendously by the appearance on BBC television of one who could bend metal by the power of thought, as well as do other things. The representative of materialistic science present admitted himself to be baffled; Occult science explains it easily – to do *anything* with the power of thought is entirely within the bounds of Universal Law. Thought is a power/force as real and as strong (or more so) as electricity for instance. In the *Mahatma Letters to A. P. Sinnett* (Letter No. IX) the Master K.H. says 'Remembering thoughts are things; they have tenacity, coherence and life . . .' We all use the power of thought all the time – for good and for ill – but for the most part unconsciously. In order to produce something as dramatic as bending spoons and forks, the thought has to be directed with intent. Clearly it takes training and practice. As the young man in question has been able to perform the feat since childhood, and many other children now find they can do it too, it seems not unreasonable to assume that the faculty has been developed and 'brought over' from a previous life.

The ability to operate the power of thought/will is shown by Initiates (Masters, Adepts, those who have reached, by their own efforts, an advanced state of being, called Whole Mind) who can dematerialize matter and re-materialize it in a different place (apports); and by the occupants of Flying Saucers who can make themselves light/heavy, meaning they can 'float' over the surface of the earth, or can make indentations in it, where earthlings find it impossible to do so (see the famous Adamski contact in the Arizona desert). They can even 'build' a physical body by the power of thought – to say nothing of travelling at the *speed* of thought, that is, instantaneously. All such phenomena comply completely with Occult law; they are still regarded as mysterious (or 'supernatural') and unexplainable by the laws of physics.

### 3. *Is the Law good ...*

... or bad, or indifferent? It is none of these things. Being of the nature of the Source, the Essence of Allness, it cannot possibly have attributes, which by their very description belong to the realm of dualities. To speak of Law as good or bad is to humanize/personalize/ anthropomorphize it. It can therefore only be regarded in negatives – impersonal, neuter, immutable, implacable; it cannot be deviated or propitiated by any means whatsoever.

This makes a nonsense of petitionary prayer as advocated/practised by exoteric religions. The idea of prayer is pernicious; it kills in man self-reliance, for he expects some outside entity, called 'god' or whatever, to sort out his problems, make everything right for *him*. The teaching of Occultism could not be more different, in fact it is the reverse – that man must deal with the effects of the causes he sets in motion, that he must restore the harmony/balance which has been disturbed by him. The function of Law is to see that this happens; it is not kind or unkind; it does not reward or punish; there is no personal aspect at all; simply and directly it maintains equilibrium. 'Nature is destitute of goodness or malice; she follows only immutable laws when she either gives life and joy, or sends suffering and death ...' (*Mahatma Letters to A. P. Sinnett*. Letter No. X)

It has been frequently reiterated that there is but One

Source from which emerges the whole of manifestation. From this state of BE-NESS come spirit and matter, life and form, all forces, all laws, intelligence, consciousness etc. The corollary to this is that everything manifest is a smaller or greater reflection of the Source, having the essence of the Wholeness within it, some aspects active, some latent, some only in germ. Intelligence and consciousness, for example, cannot suddenly appear at some arbitrary stage in the process of evolution – they are 'there' all the time. So, even apparently inanimate objects have intelligence and consciousness – not as we think of them in men, functioning with awareness – but of *their own kind and at their own level.*

Law, too, is intelligent and conscious. 'Thus, while science speaks of evolution through brute matter, blind force, and senseless motion, the Occultists point to *intelligent LAW and sentient* LIFE . . .' (*The Secret Doctrine,* Vol. I p. 139) 'There is no such thing as either "dead' or "blind" matter, as there is no "Blind" or "Unconscious" Law' (Vol. I, p. 274).


II THE FUNCTIONS OF LAW – its rhythmic pulse

1. *Cyclic Law*
One of the examples of the intelligence / consciousness of Law is its rhythmic note, and perhaps the most fundamental and axiomatic of these is the Law of Periodicity or Cyclic Law. At 'Source' level this is portrayed as the 'Great Breath', symbolizing MOTION, the only attribute of BE-NESS, which is ITSELF. The outbreathing brings about a period of activity; the inbreathing a period of rest; a whole cycle is completed, and repeated endlessly, not on a flat plane, but spirally. This Law applies equally to the appearances and disappearances of Universes, and to the sleeping and waking of an animal; to the ebb and flow of tides and to the procession of the seasons; to day and night and to the death and rebirth of men. It would be difficult to conceive of anything outside of this overall pattern. We see smaller

cycles within larger ones: for example, the comparatively small cycle of waking/sleeping/waking within the relatively larger one of birth/death/birth.

This latter, called reincarnation, cannot be considered in isolation, but takes its place within the Cyclic Law, as one of its manifestations, and follows the underlying theme of alternating rest and activity. We observe quite clearly the active state, whether the coming into leaf, flower and fruit of a tree, or our own period of incarnation. What of the 'rest' phase? Is there just complete cessation of activity/motion? It hardly seems likely. Rather is it a term of assimilation, a re-orientating of forces/powers/faculties, a pin-pointing of essentials (essence) and a shedding of dross, culminating in preparation for the next period of objective life. Again this applies equally to a Universe, a tree or a man.

Not to be ignored is that 'pause' between inbreath and outbreath and vice versa (at every level and magnitude) called the laya centre. This is the moment when nothing is – yet all is, the moment of change, giving the impulse to the next phase, and is probably the most 'alive' moment of all.

## 2 *Evolution*
### (a) Law and nature

If motion is an inherent factor in Universal Law, it presupposes change, which gives rise to the possibility of growth. In esoteric parlance, this is spoken of as evolution, and is an apt illustration of the spiral aspect of Cyclic Law. In other words, things come back, not to the same spot, but an echelon up.

The intermingling of spirit and matter (both emanating from the One Source) shows variations of predominance of one over the other at different stages of evolution. First (in any specific scheme), spirit becomes *in*volved in matter, densified down (involution); then after the densest point has been reached, matter *e*volves back to a spiritual state (evolution proper). To give broad examples of the process: The life (spirit) inhabiting the mineral kingdom is very limited in its expression. There is strength and tenacity,

and even beauty but there is also a heaviness, a solidity,
a denseness, with very little outer evidence of life (motion)
being present at all; there is no movement from place to
place; response to the elements is slow; consciousness and
intelligence are (apparently) severely restricted.

Clearly, the vegetable kingdom has more 'faculties' for
expressing the life within. There is movement of roots
downwards and trunks, stems, leaves, flowers upwards.
There is a feeling of life in the beauty of shape, formation,
colour, perfume, softness. We see a ready response to the
elements, for example in the opening of a flower in
sunlight, and in its closing in lack of light. Is there a hint
of consciousness / intelligence (that we can even begin to
understand) here?

The animal kingdom – what a difference. Here we see
life / consciousness / intelligence outwardly manifest as
animals find shelter and food for themselves and care for
their young. True, it is an automatic thing, guided by that
type of intelligence called instinct and without self-
consciousness but it is still vastly different from the mineral
kingdom.

Thus far, evolution has proceeded by natural impulse,
by natural law, unimpeded, with no interference. Now we
come to the human kingdom, the man stage.

Here the picture changes dramatically. Man has an
awakened mind principle, and this produces in him two
factors not present in the animal (i) it gives him a sense of
'I-amI', that is, self-consciousness and (ii) it gives him an
active intelligence, which makes it possible for man to
choose. With the power of choice / discrimination comes
responsibility . . .

(b) *Law and Man / Mind*

We have seen that in the lower Kingdoms of Nature, the
mineral, vegetable and animal (and indeed in the three
subjective elemental kingdoms preceding these), evolution
takes place in ordered patterns and sequences; life (spirit)
evolves through forms (matter) adapted to give
progressively more scope for the former to manifest, that
is, Nature works with Law, or rather, is a direct emanation

142

of Law, with no 'will' of its own. But it does so without a conscious awareness of what it is doing.

What happens in the human kingdom to alter the set up to such an extent? We have said that man is (i) a self-conscious being and (ii) has the power of choice, because of his awakened Mind/Manas principle. So does man function in harmony with the Law? The short answer to that would be 'No' – at his present half-grown stage. He 'chooses' for the most part to work contrary to the Law. There is a reference in the *Mahatma Letters to A. P. Sinnett* (Letter No. X) to ' . . . man, whose intelligence makes him the one free agent in Nature'. Intelligence . . . free agent . . . power of choice . . . freewill . . . what a prospect! But what do we do with all this? Being still basically on the involutionary arc, we use these potentialities *selfishly*, for personal gain, in a separative way; we use only that part of mind (the lower part) which is linked with our desire natures (technically called Kama-manas). This makes us inward turned, only interested in our own petty personalities. Thus have we chosen, up to now.

We ought to be making the jump from involution to evolution, but whereas in the lower kingdoms evolution 'happened' by natural impulse, that is, law, *now* it will take place only by self-induced and self-devised *efforts*: man has to become the Law. It is up to us. The choice is ours. The task is far from being easy, but we are each required to make an effort to make the transition from downward turned to upward focused, a change probably as great as that from the animal to the human, but *then* the Law permitted more highly evolved beings to ignite the latent spark of mind. Now we have to take the next step ourselves.

Mind is still the key – not the Kama-manas (the lower, personal, everyday desire-mind) we have functioned in for millennia, but those aspects of the Manasic principle of which as yet we have no conception. ' . . . the plane of Mentality. But there is no plane in the whole universe with a wider margin, or a wider field of action in its almost endless gradations of perceptive and apperceptive qualities,

143

than this plane . . .' (*The Secret Doctrine,* Vol. I p. 175).
So there is no limit to the scope available. Our immediate /
imminent work is to build a bridge from the narrow
confines of the personality to the unexplored vistas of
higher mind. This is not to be achieved by passivity; we
cannot sit and wait for the Truths / Laws of Nature to be
'revealed' to us. The athlete develops / strengthens his
muscles / endurance by exercise persistently undertaken –
the same ceaseless effort is demanded to stretch / advance
into the realms of higher mind.

In what direction is the effort to be made? All aspects
of mind have to be brought into play, the intellectual as
well as the metaphysical. This means deep, penetrating
study of Cosmic Oneness / Laws / Forces / Powers; it means
meditating on these concepts; it means thinning / dispersing
the garbage we have allowed to accumulate in this life and
others through conditioning of every kind, and which
clouds our auras and thereby every thought / feeling / action.
It means functioning from within-out, which is the reverse
of what our personalities do most of the time, contrary to
Universal Law. In other words the impulse has to be
noumenal (of One-ness) rather than phenomenal
(separateness).

What is the motive prompting these efforts? If it is
selfish, to attain personal advantage / powers over one's
fellow men, then clearly it would be better left alone; if it
has an altruistic note of good-of-the-whole in the sense of
realization of Unity / true Brotherhood / true selflessness
(not *just* at the personality level) then it would be wise /
safe to proceed.

This is surely what responsibility means – an awareness
of oneself as an integral part of One great Whole, and that
whatever one does, at any level, affects the Whole. There
is no possibility of living in isolation.

3. *Karma* – Law of Cause and Effect
    The Law of Karma brings home to us the inter-
relatedness of the Universe. It is usually considered as the
Law of Cause and Effect, exoterically; esoterically it is,
perhaps, something more. The word Karma comes from

the Sanskrit root Kri – to act. A pure act / thought would be motiveless; would be cause and effect rolled into One; would have no 'come-back'; it would be in complete harmony with Law / Nature; it would just BE.

No half-evolved human is capable of such an act. Almost everything we do is tinged to a greater or lesser extent with selfish motive, and therefore out of harmony with Law / Nature. We distort / throw out of balance the very fabric of the Universe – the Webs as they are called, the warp and woof which sub-stand all substance / manifestation. Who / what is to restore the balance? No one / thing but ourselves; there is positively no outside entity to do it for us. Whatever disturbance we have caused will have to be adjusted by us, sooner or later, in this life or a future one. This applies at all levels of consciousness; indeed the mental / emotional motive is more productive of effects than the mere physical action.

It is the Karmic Law which operates this balance / harmony restoring process. It does so with no human 'feeling' of rewarding or punishing; it just constantly equilibrises the Whole, working from within-out, that is, the periphery (phenomena) has always to relate to the Centre / Source / Noumenon. The law cannot be altered to suit any individual part; the part has to harmonize with the Law.

The realization of this absolute justice, this unerring Law of Karma gives a sense of wonder at its enormity, its all-embracing focus. Everything is as it is because of what went before. Each human being is born to the parents, at the time, in the environment right for him, where he has the maximum opportunities to put straight the distortions he has made in the Webs of the Universe, and to grow. Even a Manvantara (a complete scheme of evolution lasting some 4,320,000,000 years) is the resulting totality of previous Manvantaras.

It certainly makes the responsibility very great . . .

4. *Numbers / Colour / Sound / Pattern*
Absolute Abstract Motion and Absolute Abstract Space are the two fundamental 'factors' of Cosmos. They give

145

rise to spirit and substance, the commingling of which constitutes the basis of conditioned being as we know it.

Motion is the parent of the universal cyclic phenomenon, ranging from the 'Great Breath' cosmically, to the periodic activities in nature and man; of the change / growth which occurs throughout manifestation; of the underlying rhythmic pulse of life.

Substance becomes densified down into matter at the physical level, and produces multitudinous patterns / forms, each unique in its own way, for example, shapes of trees / flowers, their colours; formation of snow flakes and crystals of all kinds; limitless variations of finger prints; sounds of wind, rain, birds, fire – where does such a list stop? Can anything be excluded?

So Universal Law maintains equilibrium / harmony in ordered patterns / rhythms. Thus the relative positions / movements of the planets and stars affect the whole, so Astrology is a true occult science; the formation of the lines on the palm of the hand is also not an arbitrary thing, but is pregnant with meaning, so Palmistry is a true occult science. Likewise numbers play a vital part in the overall formation / process of the Universe; so Numerology is a true occult science. (This is not to say that popular exoteric astrology, palmistry, numerology have much truth in them, but the potential is there when metaphysics has delved deeply enough into these [hitherto] 'mysteries'.)

To take numbers, the Septenary Law is absolutely basic. 'Moreover, the one eternal Law unfolds everything in the (to be) manifested Nature on a sevenfold principle' (*The Secret Doctrine*, Vol. I p. 152). Seven is said to be the 'factor' number of this manvantara, and we know that when white light is passed through a prism, it splits into the 7 prismatic colours; that there are seven layers of skin; that the cells of the physical body are all renewed in 7 years (some much more frequently, but *all* will have been in a 7-year period); that multiples of 7 have significance in the human life span : for example, 21 and 70; etc.

In occultism, septenaries abound. When the One Life manifests, it becomes sevenfold. Thus there are 7 planes (field or area of consciousness existing within certain rings-pass-not, and each having its own laws) which are reflected in man as 7 states of consciousness, 7 bodies/vehicles (for detailed description of these see *Key to Theosophy* by H. P. Blavatsky), there are 7 sub-races in each Root Race; there are 7 Root Races on each of 7 globes, which constitute a Round etc; 7 keys are needed to unlock the secrets of occultism; there are 7 elements (4 only manifest so far); there are 7 senses (5 only developed as yet), etc.

Other numbers have great significance too. 3, for instance, represents duality and the link between the two opposite poles; 3 forms the first geometrical figure, the triangle. 5, the pentagon, is often used to represent man, for he has only 5 of his 7 principles activated; 5 is also the number of mind, the 5th principle. 8 – one thinks of the Buddha's Noble Eightfold Path. 10 was regarded as a perfect number by Plato; 12 by the Pythagoreans, each with a gradation of meaning – and so on.

There is yet another way in which the pattern/pulse beat of numbers/rhythms reveals itself in Law – in the written word – that is to say in certain 'written words' or books. It is like this. During the last twenty-five years of each century the 'powers-that-be', that is, those highly evolved beings forming the Great White Brotherhood, are permitted to make a special effort for the enlightening of humanity – those members of it who have eyes to see/ears to hear. In 1875, those 'Masters' saw fit to use as their amanuensis one called H. P. Blavatsky. Among the many tasks she performed for them/humanity was the writing of voluminous books and articles, so that, for the first time, Occult Truths and Laws were made available to the masses, instead of being preserved in the Mystery Schools for the (spiritually) elite, as heretofore.

But it is an Occult Law that the Secrets of Nature cannot be given indiscriminately to the profane, any more than pearls can be cast before swine, so the books of H. P. Blavatsky are not simple text books, which can be learned by rote; the facts/secrets lie concealed in the text, and are there only for those who are willing to have eyes to see/ ears to hear.

It is an interesting fact that the manuscript of *The*

*Secret Doctrine* for instance, was checked and corrected by those Masters – some 16 of them – every night. H.P. Blavatsky was herself an initiate; she knew/understood what she was writing (there is no question of it being automatic writing) in full consciousness – but there was something which the Masters – higher initiates could add. They could insert, quite unobtrusively, clues, into the very text itself; clues governed by the Universal Laws of Numbers/of Patterns/of Rhythms; clues which truly are discernible only by those students who are willing to look beyond/deeper than the obvious and it would still be completely within the range of Law for these Masters to *arrange* for these keys to remain when the book was finally published.

Many serious students have discovered, through penetrating study/searching, many such clues – so many that coincidence can of a surety be ruled out. This type of study is called the 'Concentric Key' method, and new aspects are being discovered constantly. (It must be stressed that this method can only be used on the *original* editions (or their facsimiles) of such works as *The Secret Doctrine* and *The Key to Theosophy*. Other later editions have been altered/distorted to such an extent as to remove completely all the Keys/Clues.) For instance, it has been said that the Universe is seven-fold in manifestation, so 'seven-ness' gives a clue to Wholeness, to extra-special significance. Thus, taking the Secret Doctrine, there may be an actual 7, (e.g., 27, 74 etc.) a multiple of 7 (e.g., 14, 49 etc.), an addition of 7 (e.g., 34, 151, 574 etc.) and so on, and this may apply to the page number, the number of the line on any page, (from top or bottom), the section number, the number of letters in a word, the numerical value of a word and so on. Such clues will frequently give extra depth of meaning not previously realized; it is a movement/stretch in consciousness from linear Western, Anglo-Saxon thinking to Concentric/spiral/metaphysical THINKING, and in all Truth cannot be dismissed out of hand by those who have not given it a fair trial/testing. Who is so blind as to presume that 4th Round, 5th Race, Humanity has discovered all the Laws of Nature?

Furthermore, we have to look deeper yet, when we read, for instance, the following: '. . . But *seven* is the real scale of nature, in Occultism, and 7 has to be multiplied in quite a different way and method, unknown as yet to European nations' (*The Secret Doctrine,* Vol. I p. 656 footnote) – and $6+5+6=17$, and the *'seven'* and '7' occur on the 7th line of that footnote!!!

One could go on and on with examples *ad infinitum,* with 7 and all the other numbers. H. P. Blavatsky herself gives many pointers to the validity of the Concentric Key method of study, for example, in her *Collected Writings* Vol. II p. 408, where she cites the constant recurrence of the Number 7 in all ancient nations/cultures and on p. 488 she gives staggering facts as to how 7 turned up again and again with regard to herself and Col. Olcott, the co-founders of the Theosophical Movement. She ends that article 'And if, indeed, we must admit that some mysterious law of numerical potentialities is asserting itself in shaping the fortunes of the Theosophical Movement, whither shall we turn for an explanation but to those ancient Asiatic philosophies which were built upon the bedrock of Occult Science?'

So – Occult Law is Universal/all-embracing/Wholeness. For man – 'the one free agent in Nature' – to become One with LAW, he must make great effort, take great strides into the unknown, fearlessly but with discrimination; open-mindedly, but with one-pointedness; must change his focus from the personal to the cosmic, for LAW knows no bounds save ITSELF, which is absolute UNITY / ONE-NESS/BOUNDLESSNESS

# The Faculty of seeing into
# the Reality of Things
## by Jane Hammond

Is it possible to penetrate the depths, the very innermost
of anything? Can the Reality of things be seen,
apprehended, *realized*? Or . . . are most of us earthling
humanity stuck with the appearances, rather than that
which underlies the appearance?

*Conditioned Looking*
   How do we 'normally' approach any investigation –
whether it be an everday affair, such as how to solve the
pollution crisis – or a study into Meditation . . . Yoga . . .
Occultism . . . and/or Flying Saucers. 'Normally' we gather
together any information available, arrange it in some
semblance of order and then proceed to draw conclusions
from the background of our conditioning. Mostly earthlings
look from their backdrop of conditioning – we don't
always see or acknowledge that we *are* conditioned, but
a fairly serious, honest appraisal of how one regards any
subject must inevitably show up this state to ourselves. We
see the world through a mind that is coloured by
nationality, by the culture, environment, the education
that has been crammed into us, the local religion – all of
these factors, and more besides, give a fragmented

150

foundation to the faculty of penetrating to that which underlies, to the *real* nature of anything.

## Can Faculty be Awakened?

What is the faculty that is able to penetrate? How is it developed/unfolded/awakened? Have we ever thought that it is possible to awaken and develop this faculty for ourselves . . . rather than waiting for some outside agency to do the job for us? Even when we take the step of looking, enquiring into Meditation or Yoga – both household words nowadays – there is the tendency to expect someone to do the spadework for *us*, show *us* the way, tell *us*. We are content with second-hand 'reality', not being prepared to do, actually do, the hard inward 'thinking'/discovering for ourselves. Surely Reality must be discovered anew by each and everyone of us, at each and every second.

Does this mean then that there are no guidelines, no gurus, no teachers, no methods, no laws? Of course not . . . there are guidelines galore *when* we learn to penetrate/ permeate such things as Meditation and Yoga . . . there are gurus/teachers in the deepest sense, that is, not someone outside telling *us* what to think/feel/do, but a signpost, a pointing of the way to the development of this faculty that is able to penetrate/permeate to the essence of things. Thus there is not *a* leader to lead *us*, but a challenge from within to within stirring this discriminating, permeating faculty. The Ancients never imparted the 'innerness', the real, to the masses – they were only shown the coverings. Pythagoras called his inner teachings 'the knowledge of things that are' – and this knowledge was only for 'those who could digest such mental food and feel satisfied', that is, those who could discriminatingly penetrate beyond the outside appearance by their own inner effort, using the guidlines set forth anew by Pythagoras.

## The Laws and Motive

To discover or uncover the Laws whereby this faculty or inner power may be unfolded, we need to turn . . . to the study of Occultism. Occultism also is now a household word. Regrettably, most of us earthlings tend to look towards Meditation, Yoga and Occultism in a personal, sensational way. We like to regard Occultism as mysterious, magical, able to produce phenomena, that is, materialize or de-materialize objects, psychometrize, mind read, bend so-called solid matter, and so on – but in a sense these are all by-products and incidental to the *real* study of Occultism. This study will lead to the knowing of the 'hows and wherefores' by which these sensational demonstrations are performed, but one of the first things to be learnt is the Law of Balance, of Harmony, that all occult energy expended in these demonstrations must be 'paid for', balanced. There can be no show-off act of 'powers' – motive is of prime importance – anything that makes *me* important, special, is suspect. It may be necessary now in order to break the conditioned crust, as it was in 1875 *et seq.* when H. P. Blavatsky was 'allowed' to produce phenomena, to demonstrate to the very materialistic western world that things are not as they seem on the outside. (See *Mahatma Letters to A. P. Sinnett* and *Occult World*). Here it should be pointed out that there is all the difference in the world between occult phenomena and mediumistic phenomena. The former are demonstrations by a conscious entity who comprehends the Laws with which they are working: and the latter are uncontrollable, unconscious and therefore without understanding of the occult Laws.

So if the Study of the Reality of Occultism is not sensational, not just something to be curious about in a rather daring, fashionable way – what is it? Briefly it is the study of the *whole* Kosmos, and thereby of the whole of Man – but a study that needs something more than a surface, horizontal approach. Occult Study is beyond the range of ordinary knowledge; it is the study of that which lies behind or within the fields of our normal modes of perception; it penetrates to the very root, the source of ALL. Usually earthling man attempts to penetrate to the core of his being by a physical-psychological-mental approach. But these are particular

fields, and thereby fragmented, and these fields are
themselves limited, conditioned by their particularization
– so there is one part 'looking' at another separate part.
We have not yet developed that permeating faculty of
penetrating within.

## Man, here and now

Let's now look at man as he is today, and see what
sort of groundwork or foundation he has on which to
build/graft/uncover this penetrating faculty. What means
can we use to LOOK – if it is not just to be another
particularized enquiry? Conditioned thinking cannot
review itself – just as a finger-tip cannot touch itself, so
thought cannot see itself – another faculty is needed. How
do we get out of the groove and develop this permeating
faculty? It would seem that a totally different state of
consciousness is needed – just as fire changes the state
of the matter it is burning, so the mind too needs a
transformation. Take a bonfire – as all is burnt up, there
is total transformation into another state, gaseous,
unrecognizable on the outside as the same matter in its
more dense form.

## Space and Motion

One of the fundamental axioms of Occultism is 'As
above, so below' – so to understand Man, the microcosm,
we must also stretch to the Macrocosm, and in so doing
there is the chance of objectivizing enquiry into the
nature and potential of Man.

Occultism postulates the Principle that nothing is
*absolutely* still, even for a split second of time. This
ceaseless change can be observed in the world around us
– living bodies are changing all the time, there is a
continuous rebuilding of cells without any apparent change
to the form as a whole, plants are growing, the very
particles of matter itself are moving, the chair you are
sitting on, everything moves. This movement takes place
in and of Space – everything needs room to be. Can you
think of anything that is not in Space: or anything that
is absolutely motionless? These aspects of ceaseless

change and space cannot exist independently, and from these two, which are in reality One, everything unfolds. Space is the very Root Substance from which all matter will emanate; and change or Motion, sometimes spoken of as the Great Breath, is the Root of Consciousness, which will supply the guiding intelligence in the vast scheme of Evolution. So in the source of Space and Motion we have the very essence of matter or substance, that which underlies, stands under, the whole of manifestation, and the essence of LAW, of consciousness which guides evolution.

Occultism, or The Ancient Wisdom, describes Space thus: 'it is neither a limitless void nor a conditioned fulness but both', it is the Plenum, the absolute container of all that is. It is 'the One Eternal Element, or element-containing Vehicle – dimensionless in every sense', 'Space or Universal Mind' – (for further study please see *The Secret Doctrine* by H. P. Blavatsky).

So Space of itself is limitless. Is Man limitless? He certainly has a vast potential within – but how come that Man is not the limitless space-being that he could be? What in fact is this thinking entity Man?

## MAN, THE THINKING ENTITY

*Evolution of Man/Mind*

Perhaps to enquire into these questions we must look to the development of Man over vast spans of time. Very briefly, Man has many many series of lives – evolution – in which to unfold his potentials – even before there was manifestation there was the germ of all man's potentials – rather like a seed waiting for the right conditions, timing, etc., to burst forth. This is, of course, true for everything, not only man, the whole order of Nature indicates a progressive movement towards perfection/wholeness/harmony. Every action has a design in it, even the seemingly blindest actions. The immutable Laws of Evolution, with their endless adaptations, show this to be so. What appears as unconscious nature must really be an aggregate of forces which are guided by intelligence – the

154

Mind of the Universe with its immutable Laws (Space and Motion).

*Personality*

Man's progression so far has been an automatic impulse, as if on a conveyor belt – without doing very much about it he has a physical body which is dense, balanced, capable of numerous activities, including adjusting itself to extremes, healing itself after *we* have grossly misused it, but *only if* we allow it to heal itself and don't suppress the workings of nature with drugs, etc. Much earlier in evolution, about 18,000,000 years ago, we, the Lemurians, had a large unwieldy physical body – hence the reference to giants. Today it is compact and refined and to some extent controllable! ? A Yogi, one who understands and thereby lives the teachings of Yoga, comes to have an extremely delicate and refined instrument through which to work. But this is not done through Hatha Yoga alone, but a full understanding and training of the *whole* of Man – not just at the physical level.

So what else is Man besides his physical body? Obviously he has emotions and a thinking brain: perhaps less obvious is his health body or the etheric, that which radiates vitally when he is vibrant, well and full of energy, and which droops when he is ill or tired. In Occultism these bodies or Principles of Man are given their Sanskrit terminology – not just to make it difficult, but these Sanskrit sounds can indicate a fuller meaning, one of depth – in fact they are not really wholly translatable. *Sthula-Sarira* – the physical body . . . *Linga Sharira* – the health or etheric body . . . *Kama* – the emotions, the seat of the animal desires and passions . . . and *Prana* – the Universal Life Principle which animates, gives life to the previous three. These four aspects of Man form his personality, that temporary part of man which changes with every incarnation. It masks the real man, but yet can be an efficient and controlled – not suppressed – instrument for the real man to use. But what is the real man?

## The Real Man

We said previously that we had a thinking brain, and it is this faculty of being able to think logically, clearly, sanely from one fact to the next, that separates us from the animal kingdom. But truly that separation makes one wonder sometimes whether it is a step forward – could it be that this faculty of thinking is for the most part focused towards separation, rather than a unifying factor; one that the personality uses for its own ends, its own survival – and blow anybody else? It's unusual for man to be bothered, concerned about the whole of Life. We think we are unselfish when we give up things (generally the ones that really aren't too important to us) for others – but the others are generally *our* family, *our* friends, *our* neighbours, fellow religionists, fellow countrymen – sometimes we stretch to earthling humanity – but what about Life on other planets, Solar systems, Universes?

What does Occultism teach/show about the Real Man, the Inner Man? Firstly that it is a One-ness, a triune One-ness. The Sanskrit terminology given to guide us to a deeper, penetrating understanding, inwards, upwards and around . . . *Atma-Buddhi-Manas* . . . three in One. *The Pure Universal Spirit* which always IS; universally diffused and yet inseparable from ITSELF – *The Spiritual Soul, the vehicle of the Pure Universal Spirit – The Mind Principle*, Intelligence. (For a fuller study of the sevenfold nature of Man see books by H. P. Blavatsky and *Flying Saucer Message* by Rex Dutta.)

These seven aspects or states of consciousness are the whole Man – BUT we have only the first four, the personality, activated. That inner One-ness IS but we have consciously to make the link, the bridge. Everything is sevenfold in its One-ness – from the Kosmos to Man down to the minutest Atom, all is sevenfold either actually or potentially, as all is from the same Source, One-ness.

## The Vital Link

It is that third aspect of the One-ness, the Manas, which links the spiritual Man – Atma-Buddhi, the Monad,

156

to the personality. Being a link, a bridge, it goes both ways, within and without, up and down, centrifugally and centripetally. In broad terms of where we are now, we are trying to awaken, unfold, make a Mind – a whole Mind. And it is this instrument or Principle in Man that will awaken the faculty of seeing into the Reality of things. (Did you notice that Man is part and parcel of the Sanskrit word for Mind – MANas?) This faculty, which has its very root or Source in the Universal Mind or Space (As above, so below), is the key to the Real Man. Why? Because Mind is not only our link between the mortal and the immortal man, or the personality and the Real, the galvanizer as it were, but also it is our stumbling block – it goes both ways – it is spoken of as 'our tempter and Redeemer'. This pivot, or vital link, needs careful observation because the mind that we mostly use is the concrete/mortal part – this includes all our so-called 'thinking', our everyday mind, which is coloured, influenced by personal emotions; gets involved in particulars rather than . . . universals, the wholeness, the essence, the Reality; it is basically selfish being concerned, either obviously or subtlely, with 'me' and 'mine'; it is interested only in the outer appearance of things, views everything as separate, whereas in Reality there is no such thing as separateness, there is nothing but One-ness within. When this part of the mind is somewhat freed from these personal considerings, the intellect, also part of our everyday mind, can function more efficiently and somewhat impersonally, and hence we see the tremendous technical advances made, the sheer brain power of getting a man on the Moon, the clear, precise thinking of technical discoveries – all that is part of the brain process of the mind, which has its place. Man needs factual knowledge as a foundation for understanding, but the brain process oversteps its mark and overflows into the psychological realms where knowledge becomes a hindrance, a purely personal build-up of what you feel you are, or the other fellow is. There is then no space to move, to grow. We fix ourselves . . . and others . . . with an image and forget that we . . . and others . . . are living, moving space-beings. For instance, don't you have an image of what you think you are (honestly you think you're not too bad as others go), what your parents are (of course they don't really understand you, do they), what your wife/husband/friend is, what a tree is, what this country is, the world, the solar system? But after all those images, has there been a seeing into the Reality, the essence of things? No. The image has intervened, stood between the real man and the personality, between One-ness/Truth/Reality and the outer form.

The mind can be likened to a Fire, which can smoulder and simmer away, producing nothing but smoke that clouds the issue; and then when it is quickened it burns all the dross and rubbish away, there are clear bright flames totally transforming the dross – the personal considerings, that mental soliloquy that goes on and on endlessly.

*Change of Direction*

So is it possible that this mind, only partly activated, (Occultism teaches that the potential of Mind won't be fully activated for many lives, with the exception of a few highly evolved Beings, Masters/Adepts and of course Venusians – how do you think Flying Saucers appear and disappear instantaneously, move at the speed of thought, change shape, size, colour?) can change its direction, have a totally different focus? Let's ask ourselves honestly if we don't think in the 'wrong' direction, has a sort of inversion taken place? Generally thought uses us, runs away with us. Some external stimulus triggers off a thought and by a process of associated thinking thought continues, sliding from one thing to the next, until it is arrested either by some unconnected stimulus that changes the chain of thinking; or . . . by attentive seeing that our thoughts are using or running away with us. That flash of attentive looking is pure energy, and for that flash the mental soliloquy stops and there is a point of balance, a laya centre in which all is dissolved to Essence, and from which there is a bursting forth anew. BUT which way? Will it be towards the personal, everyday

mind, the known, where *I* feel safe, where *I* can be
separate from you, where *I* can day-dream, kid myself
that I'm living a good life – whether good in the
materialistic sense or in the spiritual? Or . . . is it possible
that a totally different state of consciousness or faculty can
come into being: Where there is impersonal understanding
– maybe the *flowering* of knowledge, yes, but not limited
to the brain process; Where there is concern for the Whole
– the Whole of Life in its One-ness; Where there is the
quality of permeation – being able to perceive the content
of Mind, not *your* mind or *my* mind, but Mind, there
is no separation; Where the Reality of things is
perceived.

*The Point of Balance or Laya Centre*
   Now what is the factor that determines which way the
Mind, Manas will gravitate? What happened to the 'I'
at that point of balance, the laya centre? Generally the
'I' – which is made up of all our past conditioning (not
only from this life but many lives), our likes and
dislikes, pleasures and pains, our opinions, criticisms,
flatteries, all that *is* the 'I', a mixed bag of personal
feelings/thoughts – that 'I' holds on like a limpet to
these separative feelings/thoughts, to what it knows. It is
extremely cunning in forming habits, which become a
strong draw. Again it has overflowed into the feeling/
thought arena; physical habits, like the circulation of the
blood, the heart beats, digestive system, adjustment to
heat and cold, walking, etc., are rightly habitual in that
we don't need to give them our attention. But can there
really be the habit of affection, tenderness, caring; of
seeing what actually is, which is changing, living, vibrant;
of meditation!? The 'I' tries to make habits to feel secure,
and what happens? Affection becomes a little tight knot
of caring for somebody else *if* they'll care for you, and
let's shut everybody, everything else out – a sort of
bargain to make each other comfortable; the habit of
seeing what actually is becomes a seeing of what *we think*
it is according to its past, to what *we'd* like it to be, it
becomes rigid, stuck, dead: and the habit of meditation

is nothing more than a form of self-hypnosis, a passive, dead state.

So this 'I' inverts, distorts the function of the Mind, weighs it down so that not only are we limited to seeing the outside appearance but that too gets twisted by our personal imagery.

*Is there any Space in us?*

It's easy to *talk about* the One-ness of Life, Brotherhood and Altruism, but quite another matter for it to be the Reality. This requires a complete revolution in the way we think, feel, act. Occultism affirms that there is a need for 'A Mind to Embrace the Universe' – all space. The personal mind has no space, or very little space, it is limited by ideas, images, is a confused mass, or mess, of 'I's' – yes, there are as many 'I's' as ideas, images. Occultism also states that '. . . thoughts are things – they have tenacity, coherence, and life . . . they are real entities . . .' – are we limiting, filling up, burdening space with all those unnecessary, personal, separative energy and time consuming thoughts? Have we ever realized that every thought we have is an entity – we've given birth to it and it is there in the thought world, motivated by our motive, unless we dissolve it by consciously withdrawing attention from it. Shattering, isn't it, to think what a clutter we have left around and are feeding most of the time. Doesn't this explain many of the 'visions', the gods, etc., that we so clearly 'see' – they are *our* thought forms. These thoughts attract like thoughts, thoughts of the same density, and hence you have these powerful entities, visions. Is there such a thing as being responsible for one's thoughts, feelings, actions? What does responsibility mean?

*Responsibility*

Clearly an animal is not responsible – so responsibility begins with Man, with Mind, Manas. It is said that 'the feeling of responsibility is the beginning of Wisdom'. Is it a responding to Life at all levels, especially within? There is no such thing as blind chance; what you are now is the result of what you were, and what you will be is

the result of what you are now – there is no outside
'god' or blind law – 'As you sow, so shall you reap'. So
much for sequential time . . . but instantly all that was
and will be can be dissolved into the timeless in that
point of balance, the laya centre if . . . there is no reverting
to the state of inversion.

## The Timeless

Well, what did happen to that 'I' or those 'I's' at that
point of balance, that timeless, pointless point? At that
instant there was a conscious reversion to Wholeness, of
great intensity, stillness, sharpness. The Mind, Manas,
is utterly re-orientated, revolutionized, no longer
separate, concerned with 'I' – the 'I' does not exist, indeed
*cannot* exist in the timeless. Can we break the habit of
creating an 'I' as the throb of Life moves out and in of
this timeless state? ('The Universe is born and dies
countless times a second' says the Ancient Wisdom.) H. P.
Blavatsky beautifully sums up this need:

'The Spiritual Ego (The Real Man) can act only when
the personal Ego (the personality) is paralysed. The
Spiritual "I" in man is omniscient and has every
knowledge innate in it; while the personal self is the
creature of its environment and the slave of the physical
memory. Could the former manifest itself uninterruptedly,
and without impediment, there would be no longer men
on earth, but we should all be gods.'

## A non-interfering basis from which to work

As for the most part we are 'men on earth' how do we
'paralyse' this personality? To paralyse means to render
harmless, powerless, and this surely implies a knowledge
of oneself *as one is*, so that through understanding the
personality is rendered harmless. If it is merely suppressed,
pushed under, it is simmering, smouldering away
underneath, colouring every thought, feeling, action. So
we must become aware of the total field, face it, look at
it with no preconceived judgements. It sounds easy but
don't under-estimate the cunning, subtle 'I's' that we have,
that will lure you off track with plausible justifications.

Time and time again the swing goes too far into the personal, the personality gets 'too big for its boots' and oversteps its mark. All right then, what is its function?

It was said that everything is sevenfold in its One-ness, and each of those seven aspects has to be fully developed in active spans of time (Manvantaras) before they can again be One – just as the drop returns to the Ocean – but differently – with consciousness, with knowing. '. . . a physical basis being necessary to focus a ray of the Universal Mind at a certain stage of complexity' gives us a clue that the personality – the physical body, the health body, the emotions, vivified, animated by the Universal Life Principle, together with the personal, concrete area of the Mind – can be a fully developed, non-interfering basis or foundation through which the Real Man can focus, or stabilize. At this present stage the personality is anything but non-interfering! ! It governs us most of the time. But we can focus clearly – it's only the selfish, lazy 'I' that stops at the outer-only-appearance of things, and 'thinks' that's it. With a little more perseverance, going through and behind the outer, severing the 'I's' hold, at that point of focus the scales can tip the other way, there can be a moving in and out of One-ness, the 'I's' can begin to lessen and pave the way for a non-interfering physical basis.

### MEDITATION

The traditional approach of Raja Yoga Meditation aims, in its preparatory stages, to do just this. Those outer vehicles are given guides to becoming quiescent in the sense that they are not uppermost, controlling, sailing the 'ship', as it were. The 'Ship' *can* sail with the wind (Life), moving gracefully, beautifully poised, alive to every change of wind and condition, or it can battle against the wind, or yet again it can even not put up its sails and just be tossed hither and thither. But the part of the boat that determines the action of the whole are the sails (the Mind) – either the sails are working as a whole, moving with Life, with Nature consciously outgoing, or they are battling against Life, or just not functioning. It is this last stage that we have to be wary of when approaching Meditation. It's so 'easy' to quieten the outer four vehicles and then in a sort of passive, resistless stupor the mind folds up and 'peace' appears to be. There is a sort of starry-eyed 'wasn't it lovely' feeling – but that is not Meditation, positively not . . . not even the approach to Meditation.

There can be learning of how to still the physical body by consciously watching its movements, not only at certain times of the day set aside for Meditation, but during the whole day – how tense it is, how fidgety – does this reflect the state of our small, petty, limited minds / feelings? Remembering it *is* part of the whole and has a purpose, it can be consciously acknowledged, allowed to be in Law. We can see where the habitual tenseness is, without condemning or justifying it, just to see it as tenseness, not to move away from it, and in seeing there can be a going behind the effect to the cause, an undoing of tenseness through understanding and seeing – there is not a vestige of suppression in this, but a dissolving, easing out. There can be a permeating, penetrating within to the Reality, that faculty is beginning to awaken – and faculty grows with use.

*Tuning the Instruments*

In this easing out, consciously relaxing the tensions, the health body becomes vibrant yet still – like tuning a fine delicate instrument, absolutely spot on. The watching of the movement of the breath, the in and out, the cyclic movement, deeper, slower – seeing how shallow the breathing usually is and how just gently deepening the breath vitalizes the whole organism, brings everything into relationship and allows the emotions to be calm and outgoing, and not wholly concerned with 'me and mine'. Being aware of a slight pause between the breaths, both in and out, is rather like a laya centre, a point of balance, a stilling.

Then with this eased out 'basis' (rather than the usual conditioned backdrop) there can be a watching of thoughts,

163

just giving complete attention to the thinking process and letting the everyday thoughts become still, dissolve. They'll pop up again soon enough but a gentle persistence in the watching helps them to give way. This gentle persistence in an objective watching begins to bring about an inner sharp focus of attentive looking.

*Unconditioned Looking*

To objectivize the looking there are various meditative steps that can be taken. One can focus on a completely impersonal object: actually look at it, not in any fixed way . . . that would limit the looking to outer appearance only, and become dead; but a living looking without words, images, ideas getting in the way, a look*ing* with everything you have, the totality of your energy, being so on the spot and alert that direct consciousness operates from 'behind' the personal mind before the latter has a chance to interfere. This total looking is a break-through of direct consciousness, of Universal Mind which, and only which, can polarize the personal mind. In this way there is no personal 'seed-bed' for a conception of the object to take root in, or of a memory, there is no sense of an 'I' looking *at* something – there is just looking with the wholeness of attention. When there is an 'I' looking there is immediately a personal thought process looking, judging, remembering, evaluating.

One can look in this way at, say, a bowl of flowers – then shut the outer eyes and look with the inner. Can one 'see' the bowl of flowers in its fulness – the details of light and shade, all as it actually is, the livingness, the innerness, the Reality, which notice does not preclude the outer form.

This approach to Meditation, to a meditative way of living, hearing/touching/seeing/tasting/smelling begins to unfold that faculty of permeating, touching within to the Reality.

*Unconditioned 'Sensing'*

Those senses that we have, which for the most part dictate to us their wants, can they begin to function as a

164

whole, like the five fingers on a hand? Can they too provide a non-interfering basis for the 'other two' senses to unfold? What are the 'other two' senses? Where are they coming from? What qualities have the senses that we do have?

When we *hear* something, it is mostly outside, and mostly the more obvious noises. If too often things are said that are uncomfortable, or hurt us – things we don't want to know about – we can too easily develop a 'deafness' – those 'I's' are very clever, cunning and subtle. If there is a willingness to listen to what is there, actually there, there can be a catching of the sound of the wind through the grasses, the sound of plants (and also plants very quickly respond to sound), there can be a touching of the soundless sound, the rhythm, the throb, the very metre of Life. The Timeless teachings of The Ancients were presented in a Vedic form, (the inner knowledge/ knowing has its own rhythm, throb, livingness). Do you and I have to touch, tune into that throb to penetrate within?

Generally we *touch* things with our outermost form, our physical body, and we touch the outermost only, being content with a surface physical touch. But is touching really a knowing for the Real, the True, a responding with and to the inner touch? Occasionally we speak of something touching us very deeply – meaning it has stirred us, something inside has responded without any sense of self.

And how do we *look*? At . . . rather than . . into – again satisfied with the outer appearance which either gives pleasure or pain to the 'I' doing the looking. (This doesn't mean that what is actually there physically is not seen; on the contrary it is seen, touched or heard very precisely, clearly but it is not limited/distorted by the 'I' creating images, and wandering off.)

The same with *tasting* and *smelling*. We limit them to physically eating and drinking and smelling, rather than having a taste for the Real, a fully alive questing for the fragrance of innerness, of Reality.

165

## The Key

So this Faculty of seeing into the Reality of things is only just beginning. In itself it is limitless, as is Meditation, but there is much stretching, growing to be done. No one/thing can do the job for us. It has to be done consciously in Law, in Balance, in Harmony. As the Laws of Nature are penetrated, understood, so there is insight into much that remains hidden to the outer only senses. The key instrument to the awakening of this Faculty is the Mind, the Manas, that link. We can quicken the awakening by studying the Laws behind the Kosmos and Man, by clearing space in our everyday minds so that we are not fettered by personal considerings, there is then room for expansion. There can be watchfulness.

No one can actually put into words what the Reality of Meditation is – it is beyond words, beyond time. We can see what it is not – there can only be learning afresh, first by unlearning, clearing the way, truly having an open mind. And an open mind is ripe for permeating within.

# Yoga and E. S. P.:
# The Dawning Break-through
by Frank Coulsting, D.O., M.R.O.

### THE INITIATING BREAK-THROUGH

THE Timeless One-ness makes its marks in the sands of
time, notably in some outstanding critical periods in
history, where its significance is highlighted in a dramatic
way that throws into relief certain characteristic qualities
of life. There are signs that this century is quite remarkable
– being both a summation of that which has gone before
and that which is to come . . . containing as it does the very
real beginnings of the space age.

Timeless are the universal uncreate Laws of nature, and
these are undeviating / exact / immutable – so it is not
possible to bend them . . . but these laws, which are of
that One-ness, can be used through the awakened powers
of the mind over and through matter thus . . .

The critical time in the Western world for this energizing
impulse came at the end of 1973 – the world stage was
set through the medium of television for a break-through
of the encrustations of our gross materialism with all our
'nuts-and-bolts' earthy (merely three-dimensional time-
space) physics to an inner touch, that is beyond, which is
of metaphysics . . . a break-through moreover that
constitutes an opening up of the 'World Mind' to new

167

horizons, to an inner dimension of thought, and with it a sudden realization for the many that the seemingly impossible could really happen – that 'miracles' didn't just belong to a remote past – that there was in fact a power/a presence that could be tapped and directed by those with the inner know how and . . .

### Laws of Nature become Manifest

And how did this all come about? . . . This initiating impulse was triggered off by Uri Geller demonstrating telepathy/thought transference and the use of his powers over material objects (psychokinesis) – enabling watches to go, disabling others (even of viewers!) . . . such things as a minute hand became bent behind the glass, merely using his hands in relation to the objects as palm above the watch, or vibrant with fists clenched together above the object to focus and direct this vital magnetic fluid (odic force or the permeating ether of the mind). Forks and spoons that were stroked lightly a few times would bend and bend or break. When asked on occasion how he did it, he would say with his humorous twinkle, 'I say "bend, bend, bend", and if it still does not bend, I say "please bend".'

It will be seen, from the above, that the power used as such is neutral, and can be enabling or disabling, according to the will of the practitioner being positively polarized and creative as in healing work, or negatively destructive, as when there is a reactive charge of 'evil' intent/ intrigue/spells cast. This has brought out into the world a realization of the power of directed thought in no small way. Are we responsible enough people to start using this initial impulse the right way?

### The Power of Thought

The Masters of Yoga speak decisively about the nature of thought: to quote Mahatma Koot Hoomi from *The Mahatma Letters*: 'Thoughts are things – have tenacity, coherence, and life – they are real entities.'

The part played by thought is profoundly affected by the setting. What was the background to all this? . . . Take

168

his name Gel(l)er . . . was not even that expressive of his
precise function in 1973–75? Was it not a critical point
in this era of ours, when things were ripe for change and
ready to gel – come into line – and open up for new
revelations to regenerate the world – tired as it is, of
all the old-established outworn beliefs, and deadened as
it is with all its gross materialism?

Just as in our Space Age Uri Gagarin was our first
earth man to be thrust out into space: so Uri Geller is
the first to make the space inside man a living reality to
the world . . . that infinite space, behind our 3-D time-
space continuum, yet with the mind of man, that has its
own laws of consciousness . . . that work in depth.


### LAW OF CYCLES

Change is brought about by Law (as is everything else)
and law works in cycles, in its comings and goings, be it
of the days and nights, the seasons, of man himself, and
even worlds . . . and universes! Cosmically there is this
endless motion / rhythmicity inherent in every particle of
matter throughout the Universe – in the ebb and flow of
tides, of the waves in each tide, of the wavelets in each
wave and so on and on – And thus it is with the waves
of enlightenment – the most obviously persistent of which
already shows signs of reaching the greatest ever
crescendo: the '100' year cycle that starts in the last
quarter of every century, which can reach the highest ever
peak this time, thanks to the enormous development of
communications this century, and specifically, as can be
seen, the television.

*The Hundred years cycle*

What do we know of this centennial cycle? . . . Madame
Blavatsky writes in the Key to Theosophy that 'during the
last quarter of every hundred years an attempt is made
by those 'Masters' (of the spiritual hierarchy) to help on
the spiritual progress of Humanity in a *marked* and
*definite* way. Towards the close of each century you will
invariably find that an outpouring or upheaval (!) of

spirituality – or call it mysticism if you prefer – has taken place. Some one or more persons have appeared in the world as their agents, and a greater or lesser amount of occult knowledge and teaching has been given out. If you care to do so, you can trace these movements back, century by century, as far as our detailed historical records extend.'

As things in life are not outwardly straightforward and neatly cut and dried, so the outcome in some of the centuries is not obviously in the last quarter of the century in the outer world, although H. P. Blavatsky did precisely this in dynamically bringing occultism/yoga to the West in 1875, heralded by a few wandering yogis. Similarly in 1775, a hundred years earlier, Mesmer brought his healing fluence to bear, to quote the *Encyclopaedia Britannica:*

'Mesmer's interest in the teachings of Paracelsus caused him to believe that the stars influence the health and general condition of human beings by way of a subtle and invisible fluid . . . he was aware of the healing and magnetic power in his own hands, and in 1775 he first called the force emanating from his body 'animal magnetism' (prana) which permeated the Universe.'

*The Outpouring*

In the Introductory of *The Secret Doctrine* by H. P. Blavatsky, is written, 'They (the teachings) will be derided and rejected a priori in this century (the 19th); but only in this one. For in the twentieth century of our era, scholars will begin to recognize that the Secret Doctrine has neither been invented nor exaggerated, but, on the contrary, simply outlined; and finally that its teachings antedate the Vedas (Hindu sacred rhythms/works).

'This is no pretension to prophecy but simply a statement based on the knowledge of facts. Every century an attempt is being made to show the world that Occultism is no vain superstition. Once the door permitted to be kept a little ajar, it will be opened wider with every new century. The times are ripe for a more serious knowledge than hitherto *permitted*, though still very limited so far.'

One sees again how these outpourings have to operate in law viz. 'than hitherto permitted' above – there is nothing arbitrary about that.

. . . and the most heartening note from the same
source . . .

'In Century the Twentieth some disciple more informed,
and far better fitted, may be sent by the Masters of
Wisdom to give final and irrefutable proofs that there
exists a Science called Gupta-Vidya' (The Occult
Science).

. . . and finally a thought-provoking note from HPB's
*Collected Writings**

'The twentieth century has strange developments in
store for humanity, and may even be the last of its name.'


## THE STAGE IS SET

Does this not rather confirm that the stage is set, as
never before, to make a new impetus. And how well have
we prepared the way for it in ourselves, in our relationship
with one another, our work and so forth, for the new
responsibility, which this heralds? How ready are we to
receive this eye-opener of thought transference and
thought power? . . . such demonstrations are a mere
nothing relatively speaking to a fakir / yogi who would
regard them as the most superficial of phenomena in
*themselves*, but when purposively done, as they were, for
the whole world to see or know about, this can deepen
and widen man's understanding – or at least give him
cause to think for himself what it was all about; *then*
it is *entirely* a different matter. Uri has since given further
evidence of being a conscious agent of law / a mediator,
in that he has produced like phenomena in front of a
highly critical, disbelieving group of 'scientists'.

*Does your watch need mending? . . .*

How trite could one be about the 'magic' of universal
Laws . . . or is there more to it than that? Does our *watch*
need mending? . . . looked at in an analagous sense, have
we the inner note / rhythm / timing that is needed for
these challenging times, to be at one with the laws of our

*Vol. VIII, p. 205

being . . . that regulates the movement of our watchfulness?

Evidence abounds that people, when given the right lead, are only too ready and willing to 'play the game'* and start to see not only that psychic phenomena exist in their own right, but also something of their underlying significance. The vast majority can, *until* highly geared dissuaders come along, appreciate the fact that at sessions as Uri Geller's, about 20 out of every 30 watches that were out of order, started to work again, whether they were placed around him *or* in front of viewers' television screens – viz. the omnipresence of Space IS . . . and this can become a living reality to them, that can be consciously used to control matter.

Interesting is the spontaneous outbreak of such cases as the seven-year-old unspoilt child like Mark of Ipswich (an age at which a human is not necessarily too cluttered/infected by the outer world) – who instantly, but *instantly* taps this power . . . has no difficulty in tapping/ channelling this power and *letting* forks and spoons bend at his will. What sort of give has a person like that? With Uri there was talk of an energy coming into the iron . . . and the inference that space beings provided the intelligence behind these phenomena. Could there not be space within such individuals that is inherent in a quiet alert mind that is resonant with this fluence – that has power over matter? . . .

### THE WORLD MIND

So there is a break-through for the World Mind, for the humanity of our village, planet earth – we have perhaps looked on (and in?) for a few pages together. Have we

---

*The fact is that the 'Game of Life' has its own rules, which are yet exact and undeviating – to be discovered/unravelled by the inner eye of the mind; these are not obvious/never apparent to the worldly wise, who is influenced by (and stuck in) the external appearances, as earthly physics and science – and these phenomena are all beyond that range in the realm of occult science, which thus requires specifically aligned conditions to be effective.

started to make a break-through from our personal superficial values to values in depth, that are more impartial/impersonal/universal, that are in fact unifying, being of the one-ness? . . . If the idea of this at least means something to us, then there is a knowing of the freedom that is inherent in consciousness/in the laws of our being which *can* give us a balanced perspective of life – *if*, yet only if, we reflect on these matters *persistently*. Unless they are given room (space) for thought the rutted old ways are only too ready to clamp down on us, and stop that divine renovating impulse easing out and opening up right through our being.

*The Inner Touch*

The signs are here all right of this awakening of the inner touch, especially in the young – (not necessarily young in cyclic lives . . .) – with their fresh minds, at least relatively unalloyed and pure, shown in the local (in England for instance!) mind-awakening band of spoon benders.

INMETALIZATION AND THOUGHT TRANSFERENCE

Why all this 'thusness' all of a sudden out of the blue? . . . people ask – 'why all this emphasis on metal/steel involved . . . and never before?' . . . so they thought. What are the facts? – The adepts (Masters of Yoga) always had perfect control over matter in the mineral and the vegetable kingdom, and now and then they used to allow their disciples to demonstrate their lesser siddhis (powers) in particular ways . . . . viz. Madame Blavatsky (see *Occult World* by A. P. Sinnett for details of HPB and her phenomena) had remarkable powers, and she was allowed to cause rappings to occur and 'astral bells' when and where she felt disposed – the demonstration of other powers – as rendering a card table so immobile that four strong men could not budge it, or, for that matter, materializing a teapot as she once also did without a spout! – were allowed on certain occasions. But look at what lies behind it, as this is where the workings of law reside and *can* become evident to the searching mind.

173

## The Spoon Lightener

Interesting is that the fork/the spoon, that bends or breaks the 'Uri' way through the magnetic flux, is *invariably* lighter and more plastic afterwards! . . . yet *no* heat was generated in the process. When, however, the fact is appreciated that this flow is of the essence of permeability, it ceases to be so surprising, and it is seen perhaps that it may bear a particular relationship to the nature of the age. Those with the Space within themselves to awaken this inner touch may have this specific affinity with metals ('with that which is inmetalized': *The Secret Doctrine*, Vol. II) enabling them to control its nature, to not only bend, but straighten spoons, enable watches, clocks to mend themselves or break by their sheer focused presence. The fact is that Order/Harmony tends to come about in their presence as if they were suitable catalytic agents of unifying Law.

### LISTENING IN FOR THAT RIPPLE OF LIFE

Now obviously these phenomena are speaking to us. Can you and I 'hear'/ detect what they have to say at all? . . . We are bewildered, amazed, left in suspense . . . good . . . If, however, we are going to hear, listen in . . . pick up those wave forms with our 'antennae', we shall have to remain *ever* on the alert, attentive for messages . . . then our tuning mechanism can be stretched/eased out and start to pick up totally new flavours . . . other worlds of consciousness will have a chance to permeate our being. We may if we persevere – the law of cycles 〰〰 (symbols/signs don't mean one thing, full stop) we can know what living Presence is, and be born anew, alert to the new regenerative cycle of the last quarter of the century.

## The Authority of Knowledge

However, unless we remain on our toes, we may well be carried away mercilessly by the new surge of life. There is none to stay one's hand in those unchartered 'seas' behind the veiling of the outerworld, save

**174**

consciousness, and if that is not skilfully directed, and
if that knows not the landmarks and signposts, has not
the wherewithal; then great and certain will be the fall
from unaccustomed heights – Is there a safeguard, a
prescribed way that can arouse the inner knowing – the
inner certainty? Happily there is – but it is no walk over
– it resides in a watchfulness that allows study in depth,
and meditation to have their rightful regular 〰〰〰
place . . . that enables the beginnings of understanding to
be the Law, thus knows what it is to be earthed by
developing firm foundations of knowledge, that is deeply
rooted in the underlying essence of Life (with all the Laws
of uncreate nature) and to stretch out winged
consciousness in the all pervading Presence, which
being omnipresent can be tapped anywhere – everywhere,
so that in this focused state the permeability of One-ness
may prove to be the necessary ever impartial eye opener
('of the midway Round', *The Secret Doctrine* Vol. II)
free from any illusions of personal importance OR of
any limitation of the SELF.

*Making the Link*
    What will this eye-opening break-through of world
mind herald in its wake . . . Further signs of group
consciousness stirring? Obviously further use of television
(does it not give us instant contact that can make presence
physically omnipresent?) – even now there is part of at
least one family that sees pictures imposed on the screen,
while the other does not! (What wave length can you / I
pick up?) Does one not see the time when mass healings
will take place, not merely in a large hall, but with
viewers linked by the television screen?
    What do we know of the power of thought: We know,
do we not, that there is massive effect from watching a
mass media like television, and the nature of it relates
directly both to the subject and to the quality of the
watching. One may well ask how much does it dominate
us and how responsibly do we listen? . . . what sort of a
link do we make?
    We know so well that earthling man is very susceptible

to anything with which he is familiar, and so there is a very real need for care in the television programmes presented to him, that they should evoke his higher nature with more and more inspiring works throbbing with the inner note. Man has now proved himself responsive to the unfamiliar.

## MAINTAINING THE THREAD

### The Pyramid

The way for this break-through was heralded in Dr Lyall Watson's book *Supernature*, which revealed how a team of scientists from America and Cairo University were thoroughly bewildered, when they attempted to investigate the nature of the pyramid in 1968 for over a year! by passing rays through it, and found they did not behave according to any known law of physics – so that they had to give up their experiments, as recordings taken of Cosmic ray patterns were so thoroughly inconsistent!

Lyall points out the *extra*ordinary inexplicable effect of the pyramid – even when made as a model it has practical uses, such as making blunt razor blades sharper and preserving food. And do not even these amazing facts symbolize something of its true nature? . . . Do we not speak of the razor-edge path? Could its value be in facilitating and *sharpening* the penetrating powers of the mind, and also of *preserving* its store of occult knowledge as the Great Pyramid itself is oriented (North to South and East to West) in relationship to the earth with its four cardinal points. And as these are related to the four cardinal signs of the zodiac, they have a specific relationship to the constellations . . . Any wonder they work in Law in the one-ness of life? – To refer back to the words of the initiate, Paracelsus, 'the stars influence the health and *General Conditions* of human beings by way of a subtle and mysterious fluid.'

Does this mean the Pyramid is more than a tomb, or even a sign for us to look at and wonder with awe? Was it a place for initiation? (see Paul Brunton's book *A*

*Search in Secret Egypt*) What do we know of its Seven Planetary Chambers? . . . *Isis Unveiled* by H. P. Blavatsky (Vol. I, p. 296) explains that 'Metaphysically, they refer to the Chambers of Saturn, Jupiter, Mars, Venus, Mercury, the Moon and the Sun and as to its architectural symbology . . .

'The Apex is lost in the clear blue sky of the land of the Pharaoh, and typifies the primoridal points lost in the unseen universe, from whence started the first race of the spiritual prototype of man.'

How ancient *in actual fact* is the Great Pyramid? . . . Could it go back to Atlantean times . . . ? Man has now discovered/realized the potency of its external shaping . . . even in its mere shell as a model, when correctly proportioned and oriented – this is progress indeed. What then is the mystery of its internal shaping, that shows itself up physically in the Pharaohs' Chamber as extreme humidity, that is yet found to preserve and mummify dead animals, as stray cats, in its clean, and cleansing uncontaminate air? This has that quality of fluid magnetism again – the Great Pyramid being a resonator, with its own charging capacities, for Cosmic rays.

Shapes and numbers like sound (logos, the word) and colours (of light) bring us new insights into Law.


THE HEALING LINK – EVIDENCE AND RESPONSIBILITY

A reservoir charged with life like the Pyramid makes its own healing/unifying link behind the outer scenes of the disturbed world. Insight into this sort of fact is more generally possible now. So too, in this time of inner change, do the Russian psychic investigations make their impact now that the vital magnetic field of force has been recognized, as Kirlian's auric photographs that were taken in a high frequency field of one of a 'faith' healer's middle finger when at rest, revealing the clear blue fan like flare out from the finger, and the contrast when the healing work was in progress, and this blue flare glowed out orange 'as bright as sunbeams'. Objective evidence of this sort has suddenly become acceptable, showing, as it does, what is already *known* by many a healer, (or those with slightly extended perceptions), who sense, see, feel the vibrancy of the healing glow and even more its response, even in its minutiae with its myriad complex forms.

If the 'healer' is effective, he/she is intelligently trained – if not trained in this life then in previous ones, gradually or otherwise, picking up the threads of the healing art, as insights are awakened, with experience.

A basic feature, that is wont to be neglected during and after healing work, is the 'clearing up' process. This is akin to the Yogi's recollectedness, which is *used* to restore order and clear the focus in living, and his 'evening' review when he mentally focuses back step by step over the entire day's events – the clearing up assimilating process of the events of the day, that he meditatively undergoes, ('backwards', that is, oriented from effect to cause) as the day is drawing to a close. Specifically the Law of Economy comes into this in the attentive directing of forces and careful disposal of waste; i.e. bad magnetism that has oozed out with disturbances that have come out into the open – the healer does not only have to keep his own emanations/aura clear . . . (where do they finish?) – but he is responsible for the aura of the whole area. The negative emanations he picks up from his patient, he *may* rightly feel/find he has to 'flick' off the ends of his fingers, but *if* he is responsible, it does not end there, otherwise he is leaving them around in the atmosphere, where they may infect all and sundry, who are negatively susceptible. So if he is alert to it, he does his job, which is to render them harmless by consciously earthing these elemental forces, and restoring order that way.

To have the feeling for the healing type wavelength – that rippling flow of life ～～～～ requires an objective-detached-caring state for what is needed, as the *inner* well being of the patient, in a state of communication *not* limited to the patient and the operator, is essential . . . in which the air is kept clean . . . in which there is a readiness to deal with anything that may arise. This may well include violent reactions/projections on the part of the patient, that emerge during treatment . . . all of which need to be resolved-dissolved, earthed, which needs the skill that can only be born of (inner) attentiveness, in which there is no reactive 'I' minding what happens, so that such symptoms of dis-ease (what else are they? . . .) can at least come out into the open without the patient being thrown out of communication. Con-tact here is all important, so that the directing fluence of responsive consciousness can do the healing work (dissolving and unifying) . . . and one-ness is at least behind the outer scenes. Is 'healing' finding its home in our relationships to everybody-everything?

## The All sustaining Lipika Web of Consciousness

The healer, *at least* when he is working, is not unduly caught up in the entanglements of his own personal web and so he, and all who meditate – (whether they *call* themselves healers or not) – can do a great deal for the Lipika Webs of consciousness that are embracing-infusing-sustaining this planet, that has been seriously disrupted and polluted by atomic explosions, and by the pollution of sea-land-air *and* the mind of man on an unprecedented scale rendering, not only the earth's surface, but even the atmosphere unbalanced/unstable. For example, as discussed on page 107, (*i*) making it rife with magnetic anomalies whose results 'ranging upwards' cause incalculable events to happen on a global scale as aeroplanes break up alarmingly in devastating air pockets, or when 'ranging downwards' cause bridges, houses and roads unaccountably to collapse. Or (*ii*) The magnetic North Pole shuddering as never before, causes hurricanes in unheard of places, freak weather and unexpected floodings – but perhaps (*iii*) what is the most serious is the eruption of elemental forces from beneath the earth's surface being let loose in the world, where they do not belong, and bringing out all manners of surging unaccountable violence in man over which he has, as yet, no control, being so foreign to him; these also play on his weaknesses throwing him off his balance causing delinquency, obsessional states, *including* suicidal ones.

This is a state that needs regular meditative stabilizing to bring it under the fluid control to harmonize the resonating electro-magnetic field of our Space Ship, planet earth with its varied inhabitants and strengthen our link with the unseen realms and powers. Happily for us earthlings, interest has been growing in meditation, which has made a large contribution towards the openness of the present world mind.

### Recognition of the new note

To resume, we have broken through the crust of the old ways to a new look that has stretched us mentally / vitally beyond the old tight bounds; and for a smattering of people here and there to a new deeper way of looking that recognizes the old-established, dyed-in-the-wool leaders, *who* are stuck unchanged inside, are now effete, and have had their day.

This smattering of awakened humanity have, however, touched the new note, open-eyed, have lighted upon it gladly, making a break-through, and found their feet and touched some of the fluid potency of consciousness within themselves. Theirs is the basic break-right-through the bounds of restrictive conventional 'thoughts' / beliefs of materialism / exoteric religion with all their personal gods and devils . . . and theirs the right and power to open up new worlds, so that insight can be their guide that moves on ever unfolding new insights.

### The Questioning Approach

However, the new awakening is not automatically stabilized. The ever present danger of being swept off our feet, of falling for and merely following, regardless of fact, a new if so plausible, perhaps, type of leader, is *not* to be minimized. The fact is, it can too easily be automatic to be swept away by a new current, which ripples downwards *when* it uses us and we find ourselves right off balance, through sheer enthusiasm for the new impetus . . . with a new surge of beliefs, and are caught up in a new vortex in the vastly greater whirl of invisible realms, where insight is the *only reliable* guide . . . or on the contrary, are caught up in resisting it, and attributing evil intentions to the new vital impetus – like the old tune against the flying saucers, after they finished opposing the very idea of their existence with the greatest derision – said they existed but they are harmful . . . hynotists and all that skybosh – we little know in fact how much we owe to Flying Saucers – However, are not those in the front line of the enlightening wave always targets for malicious criticism? Yet, perhaps, they are 'shot down' a little less than of yore, and afforded some measure of physical protection – may be poor homo-sap has at least grown up enough to see to that.

Discrimination, the first qualification for yoga, is a long word – but it is the way of balanced insight . . . that middle way.

*Space in the Iron Age*

Opportunities/challenges of this Iron Age (technical term) offer themselves as in no other – for those who care enough/find enough space in themselves, to lighten the load for poor orphan humanity . . . if they make the grade and keep to the trail of the 'Ariadne ("higher self") thread', enduring whatever befalls . . . such are transmuted from the crude cast iron to the fibre of true steel.

On this inner side this Kali yug (Iron Age) of 432,000 years is, as the numbers suggest adding up to 9, a time of initiation, of awakening to the *life force* – Can we possibly be stabilized enough in it, to forge ahead enough, to bring our laggard humanity up through this age to grow and glow with the lighter ages inherent in it of gold, silver and copper? . . . thereby burning up the dross of its past and its backlog, which is *not* separate from ours (laggard humanity is a very real part of us too), and let all the elements of our fourfold (too often four square) lower nature go through the refiner's fire to be restored/ transmuted into their true metals.

What then of the changes ahead with the increasing tempos of life? May we be prepared . . . alert to them to move on into unknown territory . . .

and let consciousness unfold . . .

and *under*standing be the Law.

# A Focus on the Occult Understanding of Life
## by Gillian Blake

WHEN one thinks over one's life does it make sense?
Does it satisfy, or is one left with an uneasy feeling that
somewhere, something is missing? Each person's answer
will depend entirely on his expectation. What is it that
makes a course of action worthwhile? Is it achievement,
success, pleasure created or given? Is it something
personal or including others? The answer to this may be
the answer to the larger issue of the purpose of life –
underlying which may be a question of depth and reality.

1. *The Nature of Reality – One-ness*
   The ultimate reality must be at the Source of everything
we know; this would be the truest moment of all growth
or development, the moment from which all starts. In the
absence of actual proof let us for the moment accept a
germ of life, alive and pulsating, as the source. The
movement grows, that which comes forth changing
constantly and assuming varied forms, but always the
same impulse is guiding. In just this way, perhaps,
manifestation takes place: One Source, One root
substance. One inherent motion. The impulse and forms
come from within. No creator creates life, or dominates

its development, for a creator must be separate from that which he creates and in the process described there is only one life which emanates from itself. This does not mean a lack of plan. A pattern can emerge with the forms, law can be inherent in the motion, affinity can be present in the root substance. None of these is separate from life, for they all arise from the same Source. The pattern of growth may be a descent into matter, the law may be the relationship between action and reaction, the ultimate reaction being that of return from matter to source. Plato calls it the law of becoming and rebecoming. The Eastern occultists call it the law of cause and effect, 'Karma'. It maintains a focus in manifestation, it upholds a balance.

In life we see no evidence of the homogeneous root substance; instead the variety of forms predominate. This does not mean, however, that one-ness is lacking: the very quality of life, of motion – a characteristic of every single atom – can become its proof. From the Source to any focus in manifestation, whether man or the smallest atom, there is this direct link. Could man but make it back there in consciousness, the idea of minds spanning the universe becomes a possibility. To centre awareness at that point of one-ness which is present at any level in any form – called a laya centre (technical term, zero point of change) – links one with all other such centres. It is a link of consciousness not bound by time and space. Such a level involves study training and meditation.

## 2. What is man's consciousness?

Our present centre of consciousness is at a level which reacts to such an idea as incredible or frankly absurd. The occultist answers that man is, as yet, only half-developed. His idea of man is sevenfold and we are now perfecting the fifth stage, which is a mental one. Man has already developed the physical, emotional and mental desire principles, which along with his health or etheric body constitute what is termed the personality. This is that which we normally consider as man, but in addition there is the less easily defined 'higher ego'

(technical term for Atma + Buddhi + Manas). The One
Life quality of the Source overshadows man – termed
'Atma' (Supreme) – but being universal it lacks a vehicle
and focus to relate to individual consciousness. Man can
create this focus at a higher mental level (technical term,
'higher manas'). The vehicle, referred to as 'Buddhi'
(technical term for Sixth/Love-Wisdom) cannot act
independently of Atma or Manas (Mind) but acting
conjointly they are spiritually powerful.

Each individual life builds character which in turn
affects later lives. Every quality that has affinity with the
spiritual triad helps awaken its consciousness, so that all
lives can develop man's potential. The law of Karma
(technical term, cause and effect) keeps man's efforts in
balance: every negative thought or action must be
counter-balanced by a positive one in order to maintain
equilibrium. Life is a school at which man can learn from
experiences, but one life-span is too limited; many are
needed to supply a full variety. The Higher Ego is that
which exists from life to life, building a consciousness
centred on the experiences of the variety of personalities.

The higher triad can be timeless in just the same way
as the Source. 'Reality' may be described as a moment
of truth and 'real' the quality of being true, neither of
which depend on time. Indeed truth/reality must be
beyond as well as *in* time, for the reality of source, the
reality of life, is basic and is continuous. Man in his
illusion of the reality of his existence only touches the
truth in timeless moments of meditation – moments when
his focus is beyond his own past, present and future.

3. *Where is man in the evolution of Consciousness?*

To reach such moments a student needs to change his
focus. The development of civilization has been, up to
this point, basically self-centred: from now on the focus
must be on the not-self, on the merging of the whole.
Unless we understand the relationship of the whole of life
to the Source, of the unreal to the Real, this remains
mere words. The wider, cosmic focus brings a new
altruistic perspective. Mineral, plant and animal kingdoms

184

are part of the grand evolutionary process of the development of consciousness. They too contain a similar life-spark to man. With his developing mind man has responsibility, he acts with knowledge and therefore creates his own Karma (fate). He feels responsible in a new way towards the other forms of life, aware that everything around him has some form of consciousness. This awareness affects his way of thinking, for taking the occult discipline seriously means non-violence to all forms of life, at a mental as well as a physical level.

Man can change his focus from being centred in himself, to be centred in giving and concern for the whole. To do this however he needs to understand further the nature of occult law.


OCCULT LAW

1. *Laws of One-ness and Periodicity*
Two of the fundamental propositions of occult philosophy are the laws of one-ness and periodicity. The law of periodicity states that growth proceeds in cycles and that the quality of growth is change. No cycle is the same as the previous one, but is what it becomes as a result of what occurred before. Motion is fundamental to this law and is the one absolute attribute of the Source.

It is more difficult to describe the law of One-ness for it is impossible to attempt to describe something so far beyond our mental concepts as the Source, as words would only limit what is in essence limitless. It can only be attempted in terms which are all-embracing and beyond narrow, analytical interpretation. Phrases such as 'eternal, invisible, yet omnipresent . . . unconscious yet absolute consciousness; unrealizable yet the one self-existing reality' convey perhaps the equilibrium between two states. The one absolute attribute 'is ITSELF, eternal ceaseless motion . . . which is the perpetual motion of the universe, in the sense of limitless ever-present SPACE' (*The Secret Doctrine,* Vol. I, Proem) Motion in itself is perhaps the abstract essence of life and consciousness, and

185

space perhaps the abstract potentiality of substance in all its conditions and forms. There is in fact nothing which is absolutely motionless. Scientists' discovery of movement in the atom adds conventional, factual proof of what has always been an accepted occult teaching.

2. *Rest and Activity*

If motion and growth proceed in cycles then one has three courses of action: to work with the cycle and accelerate it, to pursue a *laisser-faire* policy and drift, or to work against it, consciously or unconsciously, creating Karmic delays. Cosmic motion is often described as 'the Great Breath', for all processes flow out from and are gathered back into the Source: they are a two-way flow. The whole of evolution can be considered as such a flow, or even a triple flow – spiritual / mental / physical. The cyclic process is like day and night, the waxing and waning of the moon or the seasonal changes. Just as Winter is the period when nature is outwardly dormant yet inwardly active, so man may be growing within during his apparently most dormant periods. The after-death state is a period of assimilation – mistakenly thought of as heavenly bliss, in reality a preparatory period for the business of a new life. Such a rhythmic process is true also of the whole cosmos. Eastern philosophies call cosmic period of activity and rest, manvantara and pralaya (technical terms). This is the larger cycle within which turn the smaller cycles.

3. *Mind focuses consciousness*

Evolutionary development spans all forms of consciousness from the mineral and plant kingdoms to the highest intelligences, such as that of the Buddha – and greater. Unconscious life forms emanating from the Source become densified in matter. A growing awareness develops through stages of physical density – through mineral, plant, animal and man. This life essence acquires individuality at the stage of man, the stage of the possibility of the potential of the seven planes. It is from this point in the evolutionary cycle that man has the free will to determine his way of life, through co-operation, or non-co-operation, with the cosmic laws.

Mind is the instrument which sharpens and focuses consciousness. Until this point an awareness has been simply accumulating, but from this moment on it can become activated into consciousness of a particular 'thing'. When consciousness is focused it can become creative in a new dimension, that of the mental plane. The full evolutionary development of man will be complete when the seven planes are functioning consciously and at will, when man is based in, and using, the physical and yet working in harmony with the mental – spiritual.

## 4. *The Spirit-Matter Viewpoint*

Thus, man views his evolutionary cycle, but it could also be looked at quite objectively in a wider sphere as a spirit/matter evolutionary cycle. One-ness exists at the source: emanation brings duality. It is an unfolding of the source itself, drawing out the facets of that ABSOLUTE One-ness, spirit and matter, subjective and objective, pre-cosmic substance and pre-cosmic ideation. Spirit is the root of all individual consciousness and matter is the *substratum* of all substance. Each will be essential to the other in the stages of existence, matter being essential as a basis and vehicle for consciousness, for without it there would be no point of focus to reflect cosmic ideation on the individual and physical plane. In the Stanzas of Dzyan (see *The Secret Doctrine*), an ancient esoteric writing, there is a phrase 'a mind to embrace the universe'. This only becomes an actuality if it not only includes *all* the universe, or is conscious in all the planes, but also has a focus. Such a focus might be the mind, which might in turn be described as the meeting point between spirit and matter. These two are not opposed, for, being facets of the same source, they are at root the same, but their course in manifestation takes them apart so that their characteristics develop separately. A form naturally creates separation and isolation and this is typical of the process of manifestation. At any stage it can be seen that a form separates one object from another, a rock from a rock, animal from animal, man from man – yet the essence within has the same quality of one-ness. The denser the physical form the more marked is the separation. The change has to come from *being dominated* by the physical form, as in the mineral kingdom, to *using* a physical form, as with man.

### 5. *Look Within*

In the process of learning to work constructively with nature and occult laws, man has increasingly to look within and disregard the form. Outer appearance is illusion: the Source and all that which has its keynote is reality. In Occult writings, the terms phenomenon and noumenon are used to denote the illusory objective world and the relative reality behind it. Relative reality can be regarded as something which retains the keynote or quality (life and dynamism) of the Absolute (Source, ultimate reality). Noumenon and phenomena in themselves must be relative, for what is reality at one level becomes illusion at another as consciousness is raised, and the viewpoint changed. It is only the One-ness itself which can truly be termed Reality in our scheme of things; everything in manifestation is to a varying degree illusion, an object of perception, an appearance with a temporary active being stemming from the energy and substance source of the ONE. Man needs to recognize the noumenon and to look at the life quality as a whole rather than at forms in isolation.

### 6. *Unity or Union*

In seeking the quality of ONE-NESS a student should not become confused with union which is a joining together of separate parts. One-ness always IS: form may disguise it but it is already there. The process of becoming aware of unity is one of penetrating that which disguises it, one of removing sense and mental barriers. It is not one of making links, of binding things together, but of *knowing* that at root they are in fact ONE.

Two most important qualifications for an occult student are discrimination and an open mind. The first is the ability not just to distinguish between the important and the unimportant and the subtler distinctions of the true and the less true, but also between the genuine self-less motive and the apparently self-less motive. Sometimes the 'I want the good of the family/union/nation' is based on self-interest or pride and even the desire to help homeless or deprived nations need not be as altruistic as it at first appears. The second qualification, an open mind, is required because a student must always be ready to reject a previously accepted hypothesis on finding it no longer true in the light of new discoveries. He has to learn to examine his own efforts and motives and see them honestly for what they are. Many people misguidedly imagine that they are creating a wonderful sense of unity by feeling union with others: the 'feeling' may well indicate that it stems from the emotional rather than mental plane. It may well be a comfortable delusion wherein barriers, far from being removed, have been ignored; such barriers perhaps as jealousy and envy being suppressed by 'team-spirit' or the idea of the need to 'love one's neighbour'. In the student's search for the reality of Unity, everything has to be looked at and realized honestly for what it truly is. Only then can barriers dissolve.

These mental and emotional impediments have been created during the process of evolution. The self-centred, inward-grasping early development of man's search for identity, civilization's concern for material things and the focus on the personality cult, crystallizes our separative unit and is opposed to the very spirit of one-ness. These have been relevant developments in the past but are barriers to realization of unity in the present.

### 7. Law of Karma

The third law of occultism is the law of Karma. Through the balance of cause and effect equilibrium is achieved. This law is centred on the one-ness of the cosmos. Inherent cosmic motion flows through manifestation, constantly destroying and restoring equilibrium. Actions on a mental plane are just like the dropping of a stone in a pond which causes ripples, seen and unseen, until stillness is restored.

This happens at both cosmic and personal levels. The whole cycle of manifestation is Karmic – emanation ultimately brings re-absorption, cause brings effect, action, reaction.

Much of this process is unconscious, yet once we are aware of the Karmic law we realize we are the cause of our own effects and the effects of our own causes: in other words we are responsible for what we are. The Eastern axiom is 'As a man sows, so shall he reap'. Any action, any thought, comes back on the creator, returns to its source, where it will affect him and others too. For example, a speaker, the person spoken to, and others who may also hear or be told later, will be affected; and just as gossip, or the fish in the fisherman's tale, grows with the repeating, so may the Karmic effect.

### 8. *Karma and Reincarnation – the justice in life*

The law of Karma is closely linked with the law of reincarnation for cause and effect are not limited to one individual life-span, so that one life is the result of a previous one. This is just. There is no 'accident of birth', no god requiring some to suffer, to live in miserable conditions while others have no hardship; birth and life are not chance events but the result of a course of actions and several lives. Life provides learning experiences. Many incarnations provide the opportunity for man to develop the facets of his character and the seven principles of his constitution.

Karma is not the same thing as a fixed destiny: man's own actions are the cause of his situation at birth which his own actions can change. An understanding of the law of Karma should not then bring about the negative response of a spirit of accepting one's fate, but the positive response of an awareness of the responsibility for creating one's destiny.

Thus Karma is the constant readjustment of the harmony of the cosmos, and equilibrium can only be reached by one who, no longer creating causes, creates no effects and thereby is *within* the law. This, however, is an extremely advanced meditative state of consciousness.

*9. How can our effort help the vast scheme of cosmic evolution?*

If the law of Karma is one of adjusting relationships between actions and reactions to achieve harmony, then any one individual creating and sustaining this harmony, is supporting the equilibrium of the cosmos. He has become the law. Each individual's efforts strengthen this growing, consciously-sustained harmony and must therefore help the whole evolutionary process. Man does not try to develop for the fulfilment of his own personality, but so that his efforts may contribute to the whole.

STUDY

*1. How to Study*

The concern with fundamental aspects of occultism is very important. It cannot be studied as a step-by-step process, from point A to point B – if such and such is proved then it must follow that . . . This is the way of the scientists on one hand and Aristotle on the other, the way of the particular leading to the general. Starting from the opposite viewpoint the Occultist works from the whole to the particular. The student needs to understand the relationship of all in order to place the particular. Thus he holds the view of the whole as a background to a study of an aspect.

*2. The Concentric Key*

However, occult study is more than a pure reading process. Not only must one read the text to gain factual knowledge, but one must also make it come alive by means of the concentric key. This brings a new dimension to the text. An allegory or a parable tells a story at a double level, literary and moral. In a similar way, certain occult writings respond to a treatment which gives a double reading, the obvious – and one which takes a subject at a deeper level, and suggests a quality and amplifies. This treatment has been called the concentric key – concentric as opposed to the linear approach of the

191

straight text.

Many occult keys are used in this approach. Visual patterns, placings of words, relationships of spaces, use of letters and words are important. Italics, quotations, footnotes, references and many other devices have been ways of focusing the student's attention to more than the obvious. Numbers are of key significance: the number 5 – 5th chapter, 5th line, 5th paragraph, 5th word, a word consisting of 5 letters – has been found to be associated with the mind quality. Sometimes the association is obvious, but more often than not there seems no apparent connection yet once the link is made, a deeper line of thought is opened. It has occurred too many times to be a coincidence. Page references are given, apparently to other works, but the check proves abortive – until applied within the original text when it throws up an extra mental association. Numbers have to be treated in a mathematical way, but also in a meta-mathematical way.

The concentric key is not a haphazard collecting of chance associations but a systematic collection of evidence for a line of thought. Nothing can be accepted that cannot be validated by the text, but so often the text does support the enterprise. Occultism is an exact science.

### 3. *And so . . . summary and conclusion*

Occult study must be three-fold: knowledge, understanding and action. Firstly man must intellectually come to an awareness of the significance of unity:

1. that as everything comes from and is part of a single source it has a fundamental unity

2. that there is nothing other than that single source; there can be therefore no initial creation as such and no outside creator; but there is

3. an emanation from within the Source of itself, bound by law inherent in that source.

Secondly we must recognize the occult laws, the part they play in the pattern of evolution, the necessity to work with them, and try to raise our consciousness accordingly. Thirdly we must put our knowledge into practice and act.

The serious student needs to couple study with meditation, the form and life quality at the mind level. Either one without the other becomes restrictive. The three-fold approach – the two aspects of study plus meditation – is needed to develop the three-fold aspect of his higher ego, Atma-Buddhi-Manas. He needs to turn attention from the self to the not-self, from the individual to the whole. The way is the way of Raja Yoga (technical term: a method of achieving union through concentration, meditation and refining the physical, nervous and emotional vehicles). It is a simultaneous disciplining and developing of all seven planes. 'The Way' has no concern with time and the temporal, space and place, self-concern, survival of individuality or culture; it is a touching of the inner life of the Universe, of harmony and stillness.

# Further Study

THE earnest researcher is invited warmly to examine all, or any, of the following books; the original texts, undistorted by later 'revision' are available; and to take part in a study of the 'concentric key':

*Viewpoint Aquarius*, monthly non-profit magazine, approximately 32 pages foolscap, especially useful for the isolated enthusiast who is willing to study, or even to read the papers of others; mainly Occult/Yoga/Meditation/Flying Saucers. Approximate donation 25p per issue; £2.50 per year.

c/o Fish Tanks Ltd. (a donated, rent-free address – as the entire magazine is done by voluntary labour). 49 Blandford Street, London, W.1. Tel: 01-935-3719.

*Books* (all available from *Viewpoint Aquarius,* as above).
H. P. Blavatsky. *Key to Theosophy.* 40p.
H. P. Blavatsky. *Key to Theosophy* (photographic reproduction of original). £2.00.
H. P. Blavatsky. *The Secret Doctrine* (photographic reproduction of original). £4.20.
H. P. Blavatsky. *Isis Unveiled.* £4.00.
H. P. Blavatsky. *Collected Writings,* 12 volumes. Approx. £5.00 each.

(Compiled by) Trevor Barker: *The Mahatma Letters to A. P. Sinnett.* £1.50.

Rex Dutta. *Flying Saucer Viewpoint*. £1.50.
Rex Dutta. *Flying Saucer Message*. £1.75.
Rex Dutta. *Occult/Yoga/Meditation/Flying Saucers*.
Also: Serious research tapes, depicting the Concentric Key
   study:
   *Key to Theosophy*. £3.00.
   *The Secret Doctrine*. £3.00.


*Further Flying Saucer Books:*
Adamski & Desmond Leslie. *Flying Saucers Have
   Landed*. Neville Spearman, London.
O. Angelucci. *Secret of the Saucer*. Amhurst Press.
   (Amhurst, Wisconsin or from De Vorss & Co., 516
   West 9th St., Los Angeles 15).
T. Bethurum. *Aboard a Flying Saucer*. De Vorss.
B. Cathic. *Harmonic 33* and *Harmonic 595*. Both from
   A. H. Reed & Co., Box 6002, Wellington, N. Zealand.
M. K. Jessup. *UFO and the Bible*. Citadel Press, N. York.
J. Mitchell. *Flying Saucer Vision*. Sedgewick & Jackson,
   London.
B. Reeve. *Flying Saucer Pilgrimage*. Neville Spearman,
   London.
R. Saunders. *UFOs Yes*. New America Library, 1310
   Ave. of the Americas, New York.
A. Shuttlewood. *The Warminster Mystery* and *Warnings
   from Flying Saucer Friends*. Both from Neville
   Spearman, London.
H. Williamson. *Other Tongues – Other Flesh*. Neville
   Spearman, London.
Howard Menger, *From Outer Space to You*. Pyramid
Books, New York 10022.
Uri (Geller). *A. Puharich*. W. H. Allen. London.

# Index

197